More Praise for

The Talent Edge

"A clear, concise approach to unlocking the secret of competitive advantage in business. *The Talent Edge* taps into individual unique capabilities to maximize business results. David Cohen does a wonderful job of making the business connection—it is all about having the right people in the right jobs at the right time—and how to do it. Great insight!"

> — *Grace M. Palombo, Vice President Human Resources,*
> *General Counsel and Corporate Secretary, Union Gas Ltd.,*
> *a Westcoast Energy Company*

"Selecting and retaining the best people is (still) critical to any organization's growth and progress. Here is a practical roadmap to help ensure success."

> — *Bernadette Kenny, Executive Vice President,*
> *Chief Global Sales and Marketing Officer, Lee Hecht Harrison*

"An experience-based, practical guide to building organizational capability. David Cohen shares his considerable knowledge into talent development and your enterprise will benefit greatly from his insight!"

> — *David Rathbun, Chief Human Resources Officer, Aliant*

THE
TALENT
EDGE

THE TALENT EDGE

A Behavioral Approach to
Hiring, Developing, and
Keeping Top Performers

David S. Cohen

JOHN WILEY & SONS
Toronto • New York • Chichester • Weinheim • Brisbane • Singapore

John Wiley & Sons Canada Limited
22 Worcester Road
Etobicoke, Ontario
M9W 1L1

National Library of Canada Cataloguing in Publication Data

Cohen, David S., 1947-
    The talent edge : a behavioral approach to hiring, developing and keeping top performers

Includes index.
ISBN 0-471-64643-1

    1. Employment interviewing. 2. Employee selection. 3. Employee selection—Case studies. 4. Behavioral assessment. I. Title.

HF5549.5.I6C63 2001   658.3'112   C2001-901567-4

Production Credits
Cover design: Interrobang Graphic Design Inc.
Printer: Tri-Graphic Printing

Printed in Canada
10 9 8 7 6 5 4 3 2 1

TABLE OF CONTENTS

ঙ৹

ACKNOWLEDGEMENTS

This work represents 15 years of learning and understanding how people in organizations behave and how their behavior impacts the organization. While based on my experience, this work is not an individual effort. There are many shared insights and emotions that have nurtured this work on its way to becoming accepted as an achievement that will assist others in building and strengthening their organizations by hiring right and creating the talent edge.

I would like to offer a special thanks to the many colleagues who, when others felt that behaviors and corporate results were not linked, boldly and passionately embraced these ideas. A special thanks to Jim Meek, Paul Frederick, and Milan Mizerovsky. They were the few who, many years ago, offered me an opportunity to begin the journey.

I would also like to acknowledge the support and encouragement of a number of individuals whose work in their respective organizations forms the backbone of the case studies. They took the time to be interviewed and to relive some of their early experiences. Without their support, advice, encouragement and sense of humor, this book would not have been written. Thanks to: Christine Deputy, Marnie Falkiner, Andrée Charbonneau, Dale Burn, Victoria Walker, Milan Mizerovsky, and Fran Crisman, as well as the numerous others whose efforts to help their respective companies hire right the first time became proving testimonies for this book. Thank you to Karen Jackson and Wendy Bircher for their support. I would also like to thank two individuals who, while we did not always agree, were always supportive and provided their keenest insights through many challenges: Randy Garrett and Suzanne Nault.

There were many times during the development and writing of this book that I was convinced it would not become a reality. That it has made the transition from my mind to the page is due to the efforts of many people. I would like to thank my editor, Karen Milner, for her support and passion to get this book out and also Elizabeth McCurdy and Abigail Brown who were patient with slightly missed deadlines and provided encouragement and support throughout the final stages of the book. I wish to thank Nancy Carroll for her critical eye, constructive suggestions and insight as she provided a fresh perspective to get us over the top. I would like to thank Liora Meister for her focus and dedication in making sure the process was completed on time by bringing together many diverse suggestions and helping to finalize the project. I would also like to thank Shira Balaban for her support and encouragement.

Of all those involved in this project, one person shared the vision and maintained the direction throughout. I extend a special thank-you to Keith Hollihan. He provided support and energy, always digging deep to find enthusiasm to bring this project to the next level. His critical eye for finding the right words, analyzing each idea, and rewriting provided a focus that is greatly appreciated. During the chaotic and hectic travel schedules he always found me, and provided encouragement.

This book is dedicated with a special expression of thanks, insufficient in words, to my family—Naomi, Ari, and Gil. My two boys, Ari, and Gil, provided patience and perspective. My wife Naomi, has displayed sensitivity and drive which, coupled with her sense of humor, made it possible to find time to complete this work. Most of all, the three of them helped to keep me focused on what is really important.

Finally to my parents, who have encouraged me and stuck with me during the early years of my education. Without their uncompromised support and belief that I could succeed academically and in life this book would not have been possible. As a result, they are simply excited about this book.

INTRODUCTION: Leaders Needed

&ᴏ;

There's a *talent edge* in every organization. Whether you look at a rapidly growing start-up, a Fortune 500 company, or any organization in between, a minority of people in any company can be considered top performers—those who create inordinate value in the way they go about their work. Such people somehow embody the organization's values in their ability to realize the company's goals more effectively than others through their on-the-job actions.

This book is about how you can develop a concrete understanding of what your own top performers do differently than the majority of their peers. It shows you how to translate that knowledge into a better hiring system, one that integrates an organization's core values and long-term vision with the job actions needed to achieve business objectives.

Hiring decisions, after all, are crucial. Not only do the individuals you select affect how well their own tasks are accomplished, but they influence the organization in more far-reaching ways as well. Make no mistake, each time you hire, whether you are bringing in a senior manager or a frontline clerk, you are sending a powerful message to the rest of the organization about what you value and support.

Whenever you hire talent that does not fit your organization or you choose any warm body in an effort simply to fill the ranks, you set yourself back. The result is higher rates of turnover, reduced innovation, lower levels of productivity, and customer satisfaction and, perhaps most importantly, a negative impact on current employees. Most employees look at how and who you hire as a signal of what is valued and promoted within the organization. Management, in turn, likes to support its own selection decisions by holding up its new hires as great finds. If you have hired wrong, by the time you've confirmed that your golden boy or girl is in fact a mistake, you've sent a confusing message to the majority of your employees about what values and behaviors are important and worth emulating. The organization that hires wrong pays a high price.

On the other hand, when you take the time to define your values and behaviors for success, you select talent that matches your organization's values and exhibits the behaviors that win with your customers; you create alignment between your people and your strategy and reinforce what it takes to succeed for the entire organization. In addition, hiring superior performers—those who are able to work better, faster, and more efficiently—provides positive stress on the performance levels of your current employees, thus raising the bar to a higher standard. Those employees with the inclination to develop and improve need only look to your new hires and your definition of top performance to obtain a clearer understanding of what needs to be done to be successful in the future.

Beyond these general concerns, hiring decisions today are made even more urgent by the pressures and opportunities created by our rapidly changing economy. Traditional markets are being redefined, new economies are rapidly developing, and technology and new trade agreements are leveling the playing field globally. In this context, the need for skilled and competitive labor is ongoing. The talent of top performers has become the critical difference between those companies that grow and innovate, and those that falter or merely survive. If you are in any way responsible for the hiring process, you must ask yourself what your organization must do better than your competition to ensure that you attract and select the talent that will give you an edge in the future and retain those who keep you competitive today.

Every hiring manager intuitively knows that the traditional interviewing process is a poor tool for predicting organizational fit and future on-the-job success. Traditional interviews look at what a candidate has achieved, not how he or she has achieved it. They fail to determine in advance what—beyond skills and credentials—is even required to do the job at top-performance levels. They have not clearly defined, in advance, their desired behaviors. They don't know what they are looking for.

The alternative, a behavioral interviewing system that is built right, provides a process that allows you to look at how work is done by your top performers. You can then determine what job behaviors are required by the position and the organization. This information hones the organization's ability to nail down which candidates will achieve the desired business results in the appropriate ways. Not only does behavioral interviewing improve your chances of picking the right candidate two to five times[1] over traditional processes, but it also reinforces the organization's vision and values as they are lived by its best employees and emulated by the rest.

This book focuses on the ground-level issues of hiring. The bonus is, if you follow its methodologies, you will achieve organizational and human capital benefits that go beyond interviewing. This book has been written for a variety of people in organizations. Of primary concern are the human resources (HR) professionals and line managers directly involved in the hiring process. It is also for senior officers interested in a vision of how the alignment of people and organizational values can be improved, as well as for rank-and-file leaders who want to gain a better understanding of the ways that individual job actions influence and contribute to overall organizational goals.

For both HR professionals and line managers, specifically, this book will articulate the business case for a behavioral interviewing system and provide a road map for implementing it. If you are in HR and are able to take up the opportunities presented here, you will have an exciting ride along the way. Facilitating focus groups in order to uncover how roles can be most concretely and accurately profiled, you will work closely with line managers, superior performers, upper management, and even customers. Once profiles

---

[1] Willi H. Wiener and Steven F. Cronshaw. "A Meta-analytic Investigation of the Impact of Interview Format and Degree of Structure on the Validity of the Employment Interview." *Journal of Occupational Psychology*, 61, (1988), 275-290.

have been developed, you will share the techniques of this methodology with line managers and consult with them on their hiring
needs, as a true business partner.

If you are a manager responsible for the hiring process, this
book should be on your desk as a reference for how effective selection works and how successful interviews are conducted. The benefits, however, do not stop there. Knowing how to describe what it
takes to be successful in concrete job-action terms will improve
your ability to manage and coach as well. And for your reports, the
clear definition of "top performance" will take the mystery out of
defining what is required to develop and be successful in the organization and on the job, increasing the quality of your dialogue
with employees.

When it comes to implementing such a system, leaders are
required at all levels. It is not easy to influence an organization's
approach to a key activity like hiring. Although a single person can
lead the charge in the battle of the war for talent, he or she will need
support from other far-seeing leaders every step of the way. The
process is not complicated, but that does not mean it will be easy.

The case studies described in these chapters will help explain
the journey others have taken in developing and executing this
process. The leaders I profile have shown grit, business savvy, and
determination in providing value to their organizations. All of
them agree that the payback and satisfaction in making a profound
organizational contribution has been significant.

The development of a behavioral interviewing system is a practical intervention which addresses a compelling business need,
while providing measurable bottom-line impact. As such, its value
will definitely be recognized. But it also leads to a vision of an organization with an integrated approach to its human capital. Once
behaviors are defined and proven to be valid and useful in the
hiring process, they can be incorporated into performance management, career development, and especially succession planning systems, connecting the various ways that an organization measures,
assesses, and thinks about work. Doing so will deepen everyone's
understanding of how the organization actually operates and creates

a common lexicon of terminology, a concrete understanding of the organization's values, and a shared focus for achieving its strategic goals.

You will have to build this process in the context of your organization's particular needs. This book can only point you in the right direction—you must take the steps. I have learned one fundamental truth: selection criteria designed for one organization do not work for another, no matter how similar.

My colleagues in consulting may not agree, but I believe that there is no such thing as a successful off-the-shelf interviewing process—unless, of course, there is an effective one out there that I have not yet encountered. You know that your company has its own problems and virtues, skills, and skill gaps. In fact, every organization has a unique culture and value-set as well as its own specific competencies and strategic goals. Identifying who should be hired by a particular organization is a process that must be taken with rigorous care.

The practices I describe in this book do not relay a cookie-cutter approach based on theoretical research. Rather, I give you the tools necessary for digging into the reality of how work is done in your organization so that you can develop a system for hiring the best people for your organization.

Value Beyond the Balance Sheet: The Right People

Are Your People Really Your Competitive Advantage?

Almost every organization likes to proclaim that "people are its competitive advantage." Is yours one of them?

Consulting firms sing this mantra from the mountain tops. Organizational nirvana, they insist, is just around the corner. It's easy to get there—you simply align your people with your strategic goals.

As anyone in the field knows, the difficulty lies in the execution. It takes top performers to make business strategy win in the marketplace. Given a critical situation, you know who you can rely on to get the job done. Yet how many of those top performers do you have in your department? One or two, if you're lucky. Think of what could be accomplished if you could consistently select those types of people and raise the bar for everyone else.

This book is about how to identify the right people through the interview process. It's easy to figure out who your best performers are once you've got them on board and have seen them in action.

Identifying the right people is a remarkably difficult thing to do within the confines of the traditional interview. Think of your own best people again. What do they do that distinguishes them from their colleagues? Before you saw them in action, could you have predicted that they would be the ones who would really make a difference? If you're like the rest of us, you may have been as surprised by your best people as you were disappointed by those who turned out to be average or sub-par. The traditional interview provides almost no insight into how someone will really function once they are on the job.

Despite all the slogans and PR, the reality is this: the best organizations succeed not because of their people, but because they have the *right* people. Every organization has a culture and a value set. Every organization defines success in its own terms, whether that definition is openly acknowledged or hidden below the corporate rhetoric. The difference is, top performers, the *right* people, are those who line up with the corporate culture—its values, mission, and goals—and go about their jobs with the right behaviors needed for the work.

Identifying the candidate's values and behaviors during the interview process is a major piece of the puzzle needed to build that elusive competitive advantage through people. In an era in which technological innovations have created equal players worldwide, people—who they are and how well they do their jobs—truly make the difference.

The Traditional Interview: Rolling the Dice

Some organizations let human resources do the interviewing. Others think the line manager has the best eye. Some make each candidate go through several rounds of interviews with multiple interviewers; others use a panel of interviewers who cross-reference their opinions. Almost always, candidates are vetted for their basic skills and benchmarked against each other rather than the job itself.

No matter the variation in approach, traditional interviewing is all guesswork when it comes to selecting the candidate who is the best fit for how the organization works and what it needs to do. How does the interviewing process work in your company? Is it anything like the following?

Human resources chose a candidate who matched the job description well and arranged a series of interviews. On the third round, the candidate met with the line manager. After a handshake and some small talk, the manager got down to business. Glancing at the résumé, she asked questions, listened carefully, and steered the interview down interesting trails to find areas of common ground.

After a series of duds, the hiring manager could tell that this candidate was different. The candidate and the manager clicked, and the manager could see how well he would fit into the division. In fact, she might even have a top performer on her hands, someone who could excel on the job and be a catalyst for new ideas in the department—a potential leader. Digging deeper, she followed up with more questions about key success factors for the role being filled and probed for nuances of character and motivation. The basic skills were there, the right academic background, and previous job experience, but there were other more subtle points too—values, goals, and attitudes that made the candidate stand out. He repeatedly expressed his ambition to take responsibility for new initiatives and work with a team of other top performers. The manager saw some of her own style and boldness in the candidate's approach. All in all, it was one of those positive and even exciting meetings where a bright future seems possible.

They shook hands. On the manager's strong recommendation human resources made an offer by the end of the next day.

Chances are the offer was a mistake. Determining that a candidate has the needed set of skills and knowledge does not necessarily mean that they can or will use those abilities once on the job. Impressions about character, values, and motivation obtained during an interview rarely translate into how that person will actually function and act within the department. You know what it's like. We have all had good and bad experiences with the way potential transpires.

No less an authority than Peter Drucker has observed that executives spend more time on managing people and making people decisions than on anything else. As Drucker points out, this is as it should be since no other decisions are so long lasting in their consequences nor so difficult to unmake. And yet, by and large, executives make poor promotion and staffing decisions.[1]

In *Chapter Two: Making the Business Case for Behavioral Interviewing*, we will go into greater detail about where traditional interviews go wrong. For now, I'll sum up by declaring that when it comes to employee selection, the problem lies in the questions being asked. Traditional interviewing elicits responses that indicate opinions, experiences, and feelings. Unfortunately, a good hiring decision cannot be based on those criteria alone. Despite the time and resources spent in searching out and recruiting qualified candidates—not to mention the investment made once the new employee is taken on—failure rates are high. At most, one-third of such decisions turn out to be right, one-third are initially effective but ultimately fail, and one-third are outright failures from the beginning. In no other area of management would we put up with such miserable performance.

The Hiring Manager

If you are a hiring manager, you know the frustration of not being able to accurately predict a candidate's chances of on-the-job success. Whether you're an analytic/reflective thinker or a gut-level/action-oriented decision maker, the problem is the same: once a candidate joins the organization, his or her truer set of values, attitudes, motivations, and even skills become evident and these may or may not mesh with the position's requirements and the organization's culture.

---

[1] Peter F. Drucker, "How to Make People Decisions." *Harvard Business Review*, July–August 1985, reprint no. 85406.

The frustration isn't limited to the hiring process. Ask any line manager to name their three least favorite tasks and they will add performance assessment and firing to their dislike of hiring. Too often the root cause of discomfort with these three vital managerial functions is the same: difficulty in articulating a)how success is really achieved in a position and b)what top performers actually do to differentiate themselves.

The truth is, we know the right approach when we see it. In fact, it's usually so obvious that peers, customers, and supervisors all have their own very accurate ideas about what separates the best from the average. The problem for many managers is twofold: on the one hand, there is the difficulty of separating personalities from judgments about job actions; on the other hand, we can't clearly express to others what they really need to do to succeed in a new position. In fact, we don't know how to ask them the right questions to find out if they can do the job. We'd save time, money, and even a little heartache if we could just be clearer about what is required before we begin the interview.

The Human Resources Professional

For HR professionals, hiring is too often a stand-alone response to a need, an emergency stopgap for a new opening, a new business line, another merger, or a whole new market. You know the feeling. Get me some people! It's an urgent demand. It's difficult to slow down and say, "What kind of people?" It takes experience, savvy, readiness, and even guts to put forward a business case for asking a line manager not only what skills a candidate needs, but also what values and behaviors a person requires in order to function as a top performer in the organization. This urgency creates frustration and every new hire feels like a lost opportunity to get the system working —to get closer to that goal of lining up people with the organization's strategy. Hiring should be one of the key times that HR partners with the business unit to figure out what is really needed, now and in the future, yet all too frequently it's just another exchange of paperwork.

Behavioral Interviewing: Examining the Past to Predict the Future

There is a great deal of analytical theory and research explaining why behavioral interviewing is more successful and efficient than other forms of interviewing. The good news is that it's true—behavioral interviews are a more accurate, cost-effective, and defensible method of selection. There are, however, serious problems with the way behavioral interviews are often developed and conducted, but we will discuss that later.

For now, let's consider the underlying truism behind the theory. Why do behavioral interviews do such a good job of identifying a candidate's real potential? In the words of Lord Byron, "The best prophet of the future is the past." To relate this to behavioral interviewing, what we have done before in similar circumstances is the most accurate indicator of what we will do again in the future. In other words, by understanding past behaviors as they relate to specific and concrete incidents, we find out more about a person's motivations, values, work styles, and instincts than we—or even the candidate—could ever imagine. For instance, a person who has provided above and beyond customer service on the job, on a number of occasions, is more likely to do it again in a new role.

Traditional interviews look at what a candidate has achieved, not how he or she has achieved it. Typically, the interviewer's questions examine opinions, experiences, and feelings, as well as responses to hypothetical situations. But none of these criteria provides any real indication of how someone goes about doing his or her daily work. Answers are couched in best possible terms and a game takes place in matching what the interviewer is looking for with how the candidate presents him- or herself. It's no wonder we gain very little insight into how someone will function once on the job.

During the behavioral interview, the candidate is asked about critical incidents in his or her past that are related to the skills and abilities needed in the role he or she hopes to fill. The interviewer probes to clearly understand that incident, its results, and most importantly, the underlying behaviors used to manage that situation and achieve the outcome. The answers given reveal that person's values, habits, attitudes, motives, and actual work style.

Most of us are comfortable with traditional interviewing questions. They're conversational and natural. For two strangers, it's easiest to take the most pleasant route through a new encounter, with the interviewer asking questions that are not grounded in specific details and that involve no undue prying into motivations, values, and actual habits. But, even for those of us who are not afraid of confrontation and the thought of asking tough questions, if we do not know the right questions to ask, we will not achieve any better results. Ultimately, whether easy or hard, the questions asked in a traditional interview are not fair to either party. The interviewer doesn't uncover what really makes a candidate tick, and the candidate doesn't find out what the organization truly wants and needs.

Though a behavioral interview may seem rigid or formalized, it's not. Questions are set in advance and grounded in the needs of the job and the organization. However, much skill is required to react on the spot as the details are uncovered through the interview process. A trained interviewer will know exactly how to probe further to seek out deeper levels of clarity, confirmation, and even contradiction in the candidate's answers. The resulting information about the candidate is high yield. It allows the hiring manager to make a much more educated decision about a candidate's capabilities and fit.

Not A Cookie-Cutter Approach

Behavioral interviews falter when they are not tailor-made for the organization using them. A behavioral interviewing system must be designed to meet each organization's unique needs. The general techniques have been around for some time. You may have read about them or even incorporated them into your hiring system. But merely introducing the methods into the interview process will not have nearly as much impact as building an interview system geared to the unique qualities, values, and work processes of your organization.

The significance of this point cannot be overstressed. If you think having the right people is the source of your organization's competitive advantage, then a cookie-cutter approach applicable to any and all organizations cannot, of course, contribute in any meaningful way to identifying which candidates will meet your company's particular business and strategy needs.

A behavioral interview is not directed at simply finding out about a person's past. As an interviewer, you have to know what you're looking for in relation to both the job and your organization's culture. When people don't fit the values, goals, and working style of an organization, there is a misalignment or "misfit" which never fails to have negative consequences on productivity, innovation, morale, and retention. That's why interview questions must be focused on the needs of the organization, specifically on how work is done by top performers holding that position. A candidate must be benchmarked against the position and the organization rather than against other candidates applying for the same job.

Case Study Profiles That Lead the Way

As you can see, this book focuses on how to develop and implement a behavioral interviewing system that fits your organization. Research about what works in theory lags behind what line managers and HR professionals in leading organizations have discovered through practice. For that reason, though the book incorporates the validity and accuracy reports of researchers, it relies more on the accounts of those who have experienced what works and what doesn't in real employment markets.

Understanding why traditional interviewing doesn't work and what others have done to make dramatic improvements to their hiring systems will help you make the business case for change. Following the steps others have taken in a variety of industries will guide you in designing and implementing a system that fits your organization in a way that is meaningful to those most impacted by the change.

In order to best illustrate such instances, I will profile six practitioners who have brought tremendous value to their organizations through the planning and implementation of a behavioral interviewing system. All six come from different industries and have experienced different business needs for change. Their comments, feedback, and insights, nevertheless, have a coherence of theme and message which surprised even me, someone who has worked with these and other practitioners over the last 10 years. I would like to introduce them here. Their stories are woven through the chapters that follow.

HMV Canada

Marnie Falkiner was the vice president of human resources for HMV Canada—an international music retail chain with headquarters in the United Kingdom. Marnie came into HR from operations where she had been a regional manager. At the time HR was a small department, and her assignment was to look at some of the training initiatives already in place. The issues she came up against, however, led her to implement a more dramatic retooling of the way HMV trained its managers and communicated with its employees.

In stores across Canada, HMV was going through a lot of change. Whenever a store manager was transferred to a new location, there would be a chain reaction of transfers and as many as 10 managers could be moved in a particular area. Training was a constant need, a catch-up game of running out to stores that had just gone through a bump on the road, and trying to smooth over problems in performance and employee relations.

Taking a more analytic look at the effects of such change, Marnie noticed that when HMV transferred store managers, a learning curve would ensue that was actually quite costly for the organization. In the majority of cases, sales at a store would go down for a period of approximately 13 weeks. During that time, margins also went down, inventory levels went up, and staff turnover increased.

On the other hand, in some instances a new manager could go into a store he or she was just transferred to and have different results—sales levels would remain the same for the initial period and then actually increase after an average of nine weeks. Finally, in a small minority of cases, a new manager could walk into his or her new store and sales levels would increase almost immediately.

The question quickly became, what were the best store managers doing that allowed them to have success earlier and at less cost to the organization? From this vantage point, Marnie began the process of engaging the organization in a search for behavioral information about the store manager position. This was first translated into improved training for the store manager and then cascaded into the selection and hiring process itself.

The new behavioral initiatives couldn't have been more timely. In the period immediately following this implementation, HMV went from an employee base of 600 to over 2,000. The new growth took place through behavioral interviews. During this period, the disruption typically encountered when new store managers moved into new locations was reduced from 13 weeks to an average of seven and was still going down when tracking was stopped. Turnover went from 110 percent to 26 percent, low for a retail industry without high pay. And feedback from regional managers and the operations vice president was extremely positive and supportive.

Sprint Canada

Victoria Walker is vice president of human resources with Sprint Canada—a company that is (at the time of this research) 30 percent owned by Sprint USA but which operates independently in the Canadian telecom market without sharing technology or marketing with its namesake. In a fiercely competitive high-tech employment market, Victoria led Sprint Canada's foray into the behavioral interviewing techniques needed to double its size and carve out territory in a dynamic new market.

This was no easy task. At that time, the Canadian telecom industry's (as was true of the telecom and high-tech industries in

North America in general) deregulation, emerging markets, and the scarcity of high-tech workers made for a constant battle to secure and retain top talent. In this climate, Sprint Canada did a major overhaul of its hiring system in just three months with three people on the project on a full-time basis. First, it developed 26 behavioral profiles to encompass all the organization's job families. Then it custom designed behavioral interviews for each profile and made sure that the hiring process was consistent for every prospective employee interviewed.

Within only two years, Sprint Canada made a successful jump from 800 to 2,000 employees and increased its number of job families from 26 to 40. It also achieved a turnover rate 50 percent lower than the average high-tech company and a cost savings of $2 million to $3 million a year.

What really differentiated Sprint Canada, however, was not its aggressiveness or novelty, but its understanding of its own culture and the behaviors required to be successful in it. As an organization, Sprint Canada knew what it was looking for, how to present itself clearly, and how to communicate with candidates in concrete terms about the Sprint Culture—its working conditions, goals, and values. In recruitment drives, Sprint Canada didn't flag salary or benefits as a way to attract the best; instead, it let its own employees do the talking. At one high-tech job fair free-for-all in Toronto, they didn't bother to get a booth. Instead, they brought 100 of their best employees to the fair and scattered them throughout the hall with helium balloons tied around their wrists that said, "Ask me about Sprint!" Clarity about what the organization stands for and how success is achieved is so pervasive that any Sprint employee can explain what it takes to work at Sprint and help identify who might be a good candidate to join the team.

Thomas Cook

Christine Deputy was vice president of human resources for the travel division of Thomas Cook, and has since become director of human resources for the Northwest Zone of Starbucks. In our research for this book, she has commented on her experiences in both organizations.

Thomas Cook is a travel and financial services (foreign exchange) company based in the United Kingdom with multiple units in many countries. For the work in question, Christine's involvement was concentrated on some 200 units in the travel division and to a somewhat lesser degree with 150 units in the foreign exchange division, all primarily in North America.

At Thomas Cook, the use of behavioral profiles began in conjunction with a new customer service strategy. As part of aligning all aspects of the business with the customer, Thomas Cook concentrated first and foremost on the frontline. Behavioral interviewing became the primary tool for bringing in the right customer service employees and focusing them in the right direction.

Because behavioral interviewing was used in coordination with other initiatives, direct links in organizational improvement cannot be made. Nevertheless, Christine declares without reservation that the success in hiring could be seen in the results. In a five-year period, the travel division went from a not-profitable environment to one that was making money. Turnover was reduced, anecdotal feedback was phenomenal, and performance reviews became much clearer, better written, and less problematic.

In the foreign exchange group, an informal test occurred when two sites were opened at the same time. In one airport location, behavioral work was used; in another it was not. The unit using behavioral interviews had very little turnover in the first year and profitability within six to eight months. A year later, the unit using the traditional approach had 100 percent turnover and still no sign of profitability.

Starbucks

Starbucks, of course, is the wildly successful global chain of coffee shops that started 30 years ago in Seattle, Washington. Applying lessons learned from her experience at Thomas Cook, Christine has led the charge in using behavioral profiles for the store manager position. With such expansion across so many nations under a single strong brand, it is vital to manage its labor force close.

As Christine puts it, "We didn't have good strong job descriptions—not the kind you can use to manage performance—and many of our HR processes have not caught up with the growth of the organization. So we use the behavioral profiles. For store managers and assistant store managers we've redesigned our training and created new performance reviews and interviews, all based on the behavioral profiling work."

Christine plans to track and study turnover rates closely to see whether, because of these new initiatives, Starbucks is getting better retention than its industry competitors. At approximately 25 percent for store managers and 75 percent at the service level, turnover at Starbucks is currently quite low for the food services and retail industry. Nevertheless, "It's still high enough when you're going to build 1,200 stores in 2001. If you can reduce that by five percent, you're talking about thousands of people and a lot of money. There's a profound business need there."

Michelin North America

Milan Mizerovsky was responsible for training and recruitment at Michelin Canada Ltd. He now holds a similar position with the larger Michelin North America.

Several years ago, Milan began an examination of the selection process being used for the company's entry-level engineering position. The role was a vital one for Michelin because it had traditionally functioned as a major pipeline for future managers and leaders of the company. Levels of turnover, however, were high, and there was concern about whether the best candidates (i.e., those that fit the Michelin culture) were being identified systematically. In Canada, the number of entry-level engineers was about 20 per year, while in the U.S. the number was closer to 150 to 200.

The traditional approach to selection used fairly standardized criteria. In an effort to become more focused, it was thought that a behavioral analysis of the position would clarify how judgments about candidates should be made. The aim of the intervention was to identify the best candidates, help them succeed in their first few years in the position, and promote their development into leadership roles.

The study and implementation of behavioral profiles met with great success. The organization discovered key information about how success in the position really occurred and was able to hone its selection, performance management and training programs accordingly. In some areas this new knowledge highlighted what everyone had thought but never articulated; in other aspects the information was in contradiction to conventional wisdom about the nature of engineering leadership.

Michelin has since established core competencies on a worldwide basis. The success of the original behavioral profile work done for the engineering position was one step in the evolution towards a competency-based HR approach for the entire organization. Part of the reason for that success could be attributed to how well the behavioral profiles fit with Michelin's overall culture and values.

Calgary Police Service

Dale Burns is a career employee of the Calgary Police Service. Currently an inspector in charge of the downtown region, he headed the human resources department when the new police chief, Christine Silverberg, took over the service and mandated a change in culture—a transformation of the organization from a bureaucratic law enforcement hierarchy to a learning organization that services community needs.

Although a public agency, the Calgary Police Service, like a for-profit company, had a three-year business plan. In that plan, the organization committed to four different items: to improve organizational capacity through training, development, and other measures that make employees more effective; to accommodate the community's rapid growth; to deal effectively with the community's policing issues; and to meet investigative targets in a number of areas.

The new approach to running the organization required the support and understanding of all supervisors and recruits in achieving the business plan objectives. It was necessary for everyone involved to see how their daily work was important and how it fit with overall goals. This meant gaining a better understanding of how work is done in the organization and what top performers do that differentiates them from the average.

Dale led the development of behavioral profiles for a whole performance management system which also encompassed the use of behavioral interviewing as a piece of that puzzle. For years, assessments at the police service were based solely on a list of tasks. There was widespread dissatisfaction with how well the tasks matched the reality of police work. As Dale put it, "You could be the worst cop on the street and still get a good evaluation based on doing those tasks very well." Assessment and even promotion were more based on having the seniority and the right friends and less the result of doing the job well.

Understanding what was truly involved in the job of police work meant coordinating all levels of the department in examining real top performance. The effects of this intervention have cascaded throughout the service, and the feedback and results have been overwhelmingly positive. In addition to its contribution in recruitment and performance management, the work on behavioral profiles was a great communication device. It brought everyone into agreement and understanding of the values and mission of the organization.

Abbott Labs

Andrée Charbonneau has introduced behavioral competencies to a number of organizations including, the CFC and the Canadian Mortgage and Housing Corporation, a government agency. While these organizations took on competencies as a fresh approach during a time of renewal and cultural change, with Abbott Labs, a major pharmaceutical products and medical research company in North America, the situation was very different.

Andrée joined Abbott Labs as the manager of human resources for the pharmaceutical products division, the largest commercial division of Abbott Canada. Unlike the other organizations she had worked in, competency profiles at Abbott had already been well established. They were in place for all the key commercial positions, and there was great discipline among managers in terms of using them for selection, behavioral interviewing, and performance management and succession exercises.

The problem, however, lay in the behavioral statements of the competencies being used. Rather than develop its competency profiles through organization-wide focus groups, Abbott had adopted the use of competencies from a well-known, off-the-shelf system. This had worked well enough to a point, but during important discussions about the future direction of positions and key players, Andrée noticed a gap between the dialogue being used to describe the work of the organization and the terms provided by the off-the-shelf competency system. As she describes it, "I started realizing that the managers were more worried about whether or not this fit the definition [of the off-the-shelf competency system] rather than is this really what the position needs." In effect, managers were finding it necessary to force their perceptions of top performance into a framework of language imposed by the system. This resulted in a lack of clarity—a mismatch between the work being done and the language used to describe it.

Retooling the system required nailing the work down in precise language characteristic of Abbott Labs' unique culture and goals. Doing so reinvigorated the use of behavioral profiles in the organization and led to a greater precision in the organization's focus on its own work and goals, as well as more widespread use of the human resources system.

A Vision of Organizational Clarity

As the case studies demonstrate, shifting from a traditional interviewing system to a behavioral one is a demanding process that profoundly affects the way a department or an organization looks at work. As the first-hand experiences of the practitioners profiled in this book will show, such a shift may be challenging but is well worth the effort.

Behavioral interviewing systems improve your chances of selecting the best candidate two to five times over traditional methods. Identifying candidates who fit well with the role in question and the organization's values in general has a tremendous impact on retention levels—never more important than in today's constantly changing employment market. In addition, the lessons learned by doing the hard work of developing accurate job profiles will create tremendous clarity within the organization with regard to goals, values, and the nature of top performance. Finally, behavioral profiles are not just limited to use in behavioral interviewing. The information quickly becomes key to internal team selection, performance review discussions, and even succession management processes: behavioral profiles ultimately integrate the way the organization thinks about work and performance. The transition from traditional to behavioral interviewing is not easy. Nevertheless, depending on your organization's skills and resources, scope, timeline, and pressure, all of it can be done in-house or, at the very least, with minimal outside facilitation. It's better that way. Only the people within your organization can truly discuss, come to agreement on, and define what makes it unique and how it works best.

Managers, in my experience, are eager for this shift even when made well aware of the rigor and discipline required to do so. If you are a manager, this book will provide you with the know-how and skill for conducting an interview in a way that uncovers the most relevant information about a candidate. It will also help you sell a candidate on the mission of the organization and encourage the best to join forces with you and stay. Good candidates are drawn to organizations that give strong interviews. Behavioral interviewing is a selling tool in and of itself.

If you are a human resources leader responsible for promoting good hiring decisions, you know that line managers must be front and center in the process. The proper role of human resources in the development of a behavioral interview system is to sell the manager on the benefits, facilitate focus groups to develop an understanding of how top performance is significantly different from average performance, coach managers in good interviewing practices, and hold them accountable to the process by auditing their results. Your contribution to organizational effectiveness will, however, be widely valued and tremendously influential. This book will help you to map out where you must lead your organization.

ⓔⓔ

CHAPTER 2

Making the Business Case for Behavioral Interviewing

Competing for the Best

Behavioral interviewing is a strong sell to senior management because it addresses two fundamental employment needs that are even more critical in the circumstances we face today.

Firstly, how do we get the best people? In this time of rapid economic change and fluctuating employment levels, this has never been so difficult. Unfortunately, it's also never been so necessary. Organizations no longer have the time, resources, and flexibility to coax nascent talent while shedding the employees who fail to make a strong positive impact. The financial and competitive hit is too hard, and the opportunity costs too high. With significant growth levels and new markets developing every day, a company that can identify and recruit more top performers from the outset has a tremendous advantage over any competitor. As we've already mentioned, behavioral interviewing increases the odds of hiring the right people by two to five times.

Secondly, keeping the best people is another pressing competitive and economic issue. We're moving rapidly into an era of free agency. It's no longer uncommon for highly skilled contributors to go wherever their talents are appreciated. In fact, there are so many employment options available in some industries that hanging onto even average performers can seem like a heroic cause.

Yet, in spite of, or perhaps because of this pressure, low retention rates are still an indelible sign of poor recruitment. Employees who are a good fit for an organization are reluctant to leave it no matter what enticing rewards are dangled by a competitor. In the next chapter (*Chapter 3: The Organization, the Job, and the Candidate: The Right Fit*) we'll discuss just how important organizational fit is in an employee's decision to stay at one company instead of leaving for another. For the time being, however, it's obvious that losing talent to a competitor is a tremendous blow. Not only have your training resources been wasted and your replacement costs increased substantially, but you've just seen your intellectual capital get into its car, drive down the highway, and pull into your competitor's parking lot to be greeted warmly.

In this chapter we will shine a bright light on the failings of the traditional interview; then we will show how our case study practitioners defined a convincing bottom-line argument to gain buy-in and support for the development of behavioral interviewing systems in their organizations.

Why Hiring Decisions Fail

To understand why behavioral interview questions are better, it's necessary to first show where traditional interviews go wrong.

What are the elements relied upon in the traditional process? We've got the job description, the collection of résumés, and the interview as broad categories. Within the interview itself we are concerned with credentials, experience, and accomplishments as well as less tangible indicators like attitude, approach, motives, and goals. Finally, we make the decision. Typically, hiring decisions are driven by a comparison of all candidates' answers, the needs of the position, overall impressions, and salary requirements. Ultimately, the process is considered a success if we've confidently identified the knock-out candidates and convinced them to come on board. A truer measurement, of course, can only be obtained over time. Have the knock-out candidates really become top performers? Did they stay long enough to pay their way and make a significant difference?

Let's look at the issues in the traditional interview process step by step and see where the holes lie.

The Job Description

The job description, of course, focuses on the position. It does so primarily by outlining the technical requirements of the role, including years of experience, skills and academic training, or credentials. The other thing we often call for in the ad is a specific attitude. We say that we're looking for a team player or a can-do person, an aggressive seller or a deal maker—oh, and better make that an out-of-the-box thinker with an entrepreneurial spirit, too!

It's difficult to distinguish what we are really looking for by the language that we use. What we end up providing is less an indication of what the position needs than a road map for how to adjust a résumé and craft a cover letter. Certain credentials get emphasized over others, and whatever out-of-the-box, can-do, team-player, self-starter spirit the job applicant has ever exhibited gets dug up and dusted off to be placed front and center as that person's core defining characteristic.

Of course, these are baseline technical considerations involved in almost any job. A dentist can't just step into eye surgery, nor can a recent engineering graduate effectively handle a complex schedule of multiple projects and project leaders right away. Nevertheless, we define positions using such general conditions and mistakenly think that we will then be able to step up our selection decision with a different set of requirements—perhaps the real, though implicit and unspoken, needs of the position. In other words, we ask about team spirit but really want a specific brand of team spirit we haven't yet defined; we say that we require a high school diploma but really need someone who demonstrates the ability to learn new skills in hands-on ways during the workday. It is virtually impossible to find what we are looking for when we can't define it concretely.

I think of a well-written job advertisement I was shown by one of my clients, a firm that was searching for a new vice president of software marketing. The ad clearly described the issues involved in developing marketing strategy and declared that the position required 10 years' previous experience, a graduate degree in management, and a strong focus on developing market share.

"What do you think?" he asked me. "Is that going to pick a winner or what?"

This was a few years back and I had just begun to work with the client. Nevertheless, I could see that my basic message was not getting through.

"Looks good," I said. "Too bad you can't hire Bill Gates though."

"What do you mean?" he asked, confused.

"Well, Bill Gates only has nine years experience and he was a college dropout."

Of course, none of the rest of us would make a mistake like that. If Bill Gates walked in the door, we'd hire him in a second. But would we recognize him? Would we know what he could do for our organization? Would we even want him if we knew what skills the position really required?

My point, then and now, is simply that focusing on criteria like years of experience, training credentials, and academic record can put too much emphasis on factors that aren't as important as the ones that really indicate success. It's what's done with a degree or a training certificate, an internship or an apprenticeship that counts. After all, the person who graduates at the bottom of the class in medical school is still referred to as "Doctor."

Some companies in competitive employment markets understand this and take full advantage of it. There are very smart companies that hire MBAs from tier-two B-schools, because they know what they are looking for, know how to identify the right candidate, and they can get that top performer more cheaply when he or she graduates from a school that is not ranked in the top 10.

The discipline of developing a behavioral profile for a specific position will help you use the job description as a more effective tool to develop a strong pool of suitable candidates.

The Résumé

An intelligent applicant uses the information given in a job description or employment ad to tailor his or her résumé as closely as possible to the needs of the position. I think we all know this instinctively. After all, how much time do we spend looking at résumés? Typically a glance will do. We sort them into three piles based on whether we like or dislike what they say. The first pile becomes the group of résumés that will be called up for an interview. The second pile are back-ups, and the third pile is trash. The résumés in the second pile get that nice form letter that says, "We have received your résumé. Thank you very much. At this point in time there are no positions available which meet your experience. We will keep your résumé on file, however, for six months." Then we put those résumés in the tracking system and forget about them.

Résumé writing is a skill, and too often a striking résumé tells you only that the candidate is particularly good at it. After all, courses and career centers are geared towards making a candidate as appealing as possible. The workshop "How To Write A Killer Résumé" is always full.

Nor are résumés always an accurate or honest account of what an applicant has actually done. Shockingly, some of the best fiction ever written gets composed on the pages of a résumé. According to this recent article in the *Toronto Star*:

Employee screening companies say employers stopped relying on résumés to evaluate potential employees because people often fill their résumés with lies. Studies have found that more than 70 percent of business owners in the United States believe most résumés are filled with inaccuracies benefiting applicants.

Officials at Investigations Specialists Inc. in Winter Park, Florida, said company records show that 80 percent of all applicants are falsified, whether intentional or not. One recent study shows 25 percent of job applicants claimed to have MBAs they never received. "We are seeing an increase in the number of fraudulent educational credentials," said Larry Craft, owner of Datacheck Co. in Bradentown, Florida.[1]

If we really know what we are looking for in a position, we can see past the bells and whistles in a résumé and even the lies. If we don't, then it becomes much harder to know whether a candidate's offerings meet the needs of the organization.

Technical Credentials

Most of the information we need to know about a candidate's technical abilities and credentials are revealed in the résumé itself; nevertheless, we spend a considerable amount of time during the actual interview rehashing it. That usually indicates that we are going through the résumé for the first time in front of the candidate, ticking off a mental checklist while we compose questions related to that person's background.

Behavioral interviews spend very little time focusing on technical credentials. A candidate who is ready for a behavioral interview has already been thoroughly vetted for his or her baseline skills and training or academic achievements. The behavioral interview is interested in an entirely different level of information that can only be exposed through precise questions and highly probed answers.

Experience

Questions about experience provide an opportunity to unearth information unique to the candidate that can be helpful in making a selection decision. Usually when we ask about experience, we

---

[1] *The Toronto Star*, Monday, February 6, 1995.

focus on duties and responsibilities in a previous position and move on to a discussion about accomplishments and achievements. If we come up with something interesting, we might talk about the challenges encountered along the way.

That kind of information can help produce a picture of what the candidate has done in the past and thus can be a useful guide in pointing out specific areas where performance was key. Yet, significant drawbacks remain:

- Discussions won't provide any information as to how well the candidate performed the task or duty described
- Behaviors involved in performing that task may not have anything to do with what is needed for the role that needs to be filled
- Assumptions that the candidate has indeed done what he or she told you about when, in fact, the candidate may not have or may have played a lesser role than he or she would have you think

Behavioral interviews are all about experience, but the questions focus on specific "critical" incidents whose basic theme is determined in advance. The candidate is prompted for more and more detail until the incident is thoroughly fleshed out, it's like a movie both interviewer and candidate can see playing before them. The specific details of what a candidate did in the situation provide a concrete description of their challenges, the hard facts of their accomplishments, and the essence of their motivations.

Hypothetical Situations and Opinions

We ask candidates about their opinions and intentions in order to learn more about their character and to guess how they would perform in hypothetical job-related situations. For example:

"What did you like about your last position?"
"What are your strengths as a team leader?"
"What would you do if sales numbers were down and your colleagues were underperforming?"

Unfortunately, questions about opinions or hypothetical situations allow for a potentially large gap between what would really happen and what the candidate or the interviewer would like to have happen. This allows both interviewer and candidate to make many assumptions without hard evidence. The candidate may know how best to approach a situation but fail to do so when the real test comes. He or she may make eloquent claims about teamwork or leadership, diligence or innovative thinking, but not truly value those points when it counts.

The value of such questioning is that it can suggest areas where more concrete behavioral information should be dug up. It can also provide a sense of what the candidate thinks, at least explicitly. But, again, the malleability is too great. We all know that there is often a big difference between what someone says they do and what they will do, what they think is right and how they actually respond during a moment of truth.

Behavioral interviewing goes a long way towards eliminating that uncertainty by pinning the candidate down to specific examples of what they actually did do in the past. It deliberately seeks out other examples to corroborate those findings and even looks for contradictory evidence as a way of developing a realistic picture of that person's performance and tendencies.

Behavioral Information

Even traditional interviews usually incorporate some amount of inquiry into behavioral information. Compared to a true behavioral interview, however, the proportion of time spent on behavioral questions is considerably less, and the direction of the questioning may or may not have any relevance to the position.

In brief, behavioral information is concerned with specific events in an applicant's past that were somehow critical moments indicative of key decisions and actions. Behavioral questions typically focus on a person's extreme moments, his or her biggest challenge, hardest problem, most frustrating customer, and then dig in for rich information.

For example:

1. Describe the most successful project you designed.
   - What was your input to the design?
   - What feedback did you receive?

2. Tell me about your most difficult client interview.
   - How did you prepare?
   - How did you respond to the client's concerns?

3. Describe a time when you noticed the early warning signs of a problem that would have cost a lot of money if not detected.
   - What first steps did you take to correct the problem?
   - How much time did it take?

The information from these questions puts the interviewer in a position to independently assess the candidate's qualifications. It's almost as if the interviewer is watching a candidate perform in the workplace. Behavioral information allows you to understand that person's actual behaviors based on real-life situations. You can measure someone by his or her real results.

Stories about a candidate's own life allow that person to elaborate in concrete terms about what makes him or her capable of getting a job done. For top performers it is very satisfying to be able to describe the background and context of an accomplishment. For someone wishing to present him- or herself as something he or she is not, telling a story with specific details makes it remarkably difficult to mask motivations and attitudes or to hide real behaviors.

Comparing Types of Information

We've discussed technical credentials, experience, opinions, and behavioral information and their relative worth. In practice, both behavioral and traditional interviews rely on a mix of these types of information. The difference is in the proportion of the mix. In behavioral interviews the focus shifts from being heavily weighted on opinions, experience, and credentials to relying considerably on information gained from behavioral questions. The following chart provides a good snapshot comparison.

Percentage of Interview Time versus Type of Question[2]		
	Traditional Interview	Behavioral Interview
Credentials & Technical	15	4
Experience	32	40
Opinions / Situational	48	23
Behavioral	5	33

It is recommended that at least 30 to 40 percent of the information gathered in an interview be focused on behaviors. This will provide the foundation for gaining the highest accuracy in predicting the best candidate for the job.

The Interviewing Skills of the Candidate

There are two problems when judging people within the confines of a traditional interview. As with writing résumés, giving good interviews is a skill unto itself; it is difficult to separate impressions of personality from the actual content of the candidate's answers.

Beyond issues of physical appearance, gender, or racial bias, there are more subtle forms of prejudice at work in an interview. People who are poised and pleasing to be with, able to think quickly, and speak lucidly appear more highly competent and suited to an organization, particularly when questions about opinions, experience, or intentions are asked. It's difficult to overcome such impressions and be objective.

On top of that, a candidate with high emotional intelligence will quickly read an interviewer's true sympathies and areas of interest and tailor his or her answers accordingly. The ability to make a personal connection with the interviewer dramatically increases the chances of being viewed as a positive addition to the organization, whether or not the candidate has the right capabilities.

[2] William Wiesner "A Meta-analytic Investigation of the Impact of Interview Format and Degree of Structure on the Validity of the Employment Interview," *Journal of Occupational Psychology*, 61 (1988): 1–16.

It's human nature to hire in our own image, but doing so will probably not secure the right candidate. Fortunately, behavioral interviewing forces us to suspend judgment of the candidate until that person's answers (recorded in detailed notes) are reviewed and judged against the profile of the job. This is a key point, since many decisions fail when candidates are usually compared against each other. In the event that a good fit is not found, hiring the best of the bunch is no solution. The right hiring decision in this situation is to continue the search.

Another frequent complaint I hear from seasoned hiring managers is that candidates, in general, are better at answering questions than interviewers are at asking them. This should not come as a surprise. Everyone has been schooled in how to answer typical interviewing questions. Every university's employment center trains graduates in how to interview well. Plenty of books map the ground as thoroughly as a battlefield. A new one I recently encountered, *101 Great Answers to the Toughest Interview Questions*[3], surprised me not because of its subject matter but because of how good those 101 answers were. Most interview questions, after all, have well conditioned responses. "What are your likes and dislikes?" "Why do you want this position?" "Why are you leaving your current organization?" "Please explain the gap in your résumé." All of these areas of inquiry can be anticipated and prepared for in advance. How many of us, after all, have ever heard of a weakness that was actually a weakness? "Oh, you're a workaholic who finds it difficult to tear himself away from the office? Well, you'll work out just fine in this company!"

The Time It Takes for a Decision

Even with the most rigorous and insightful questions, the decision to hire or not to hire is still an impulsive one. Without being forced to pause for a careful evaluation of the information derived from the interview, the decision-making process in a traditional interview comes down to the most basic instinctive response. How long do you think it actually takes?

[3] Ron Fry, *101 Great Answers to the Toughest Interview Questions*, 4th Edition.

Most research shows that the decision whether or not to hire someone is made in the first 90 seconds of the interview. The countdown begins from the moment the candidate and the interviewer introduce themselves. My view is that the decision comes even more quickly than that, within nanoseconds, during the handshake and initial eye contact, despite the in-depth nature of the interview itself or the number or type of questions. Without restrictions, guidelines, and criteria which are core to the behavioral interview and force a more analytical evaluation, one human being decides within the blink of an eye whether another one belongs in his or her tribe. The rest of the interview is spent rationalizing that gut reaction, justifying the choice, searching out information that backs up what is already clear to the person doing the interviewing: I want this person on my team or I don't. To move beyond first impressions to a more considered approach, behavioral interviewing makes us more analytical and less reactive. It provides the framework to move beyond our first impressions to a more considered approach.

Reference Checks

Finally, the reference check is another underutilized stage of the traditional interview. After the interview is over, we typically vet a candidate to ensure that he or she does indeed have the experience, training, or responsibilities he or she claims. Unless contrary information is volunteered outright by the reference, legal restrictions refrain us from asking in great detail about a person's real attributes, attitudes, or even the terms under which he or she left the last organization. Also, if a candidate is interviewing for a new position while still employed he or she may ask that the supervisor or colleague not be contacted.

As such, reference checks are a lost opportunity to obtain additional high quality information. In a behavioral interview, reference checks can be related to a specific incident discussed in the interview and accordingly can provide yet another telling perspective of the candidate's role and behaviors. Because of something called the "transferability of behaviors" which we will discuss later, the critical incident in question doesn't need to have taken place in the candidate's current employment situation.

Structured and Unstructured Interviews

A traditional interview is considered unstructured because the event is ad hoc and the questions themselves are random. Given a different candidate or a different interviewer, the questions would change, even though the job being interviewed for remains the same. This technique is relied upon by so many companies because it is fast and easy and allows a natural interaction to take place between the interviewer and the candidate. The mistaken assumption underlying this approach is that the best way to judge interpersonal skills and character (and thus the ability to succeed on the job) is to have a one-on-one conversation in which matters of importance are discussed and probed.

A structured interview is one in which a thorough job analysis is done, the same base questions are asked of all candidates, and the answers are rated systematically to determine the best candidate measured against the needs of the job rather than in comparison to the other candidates. Though not all structured processes are the same, the research shows that any attempt at increasing structure increases the chances of picking a better applicant.[4]

Of structured approaches, the two most significant off-shoots are the behavioral interview and the situational interview. In a situational interview, the interviewer asks deliberate, planned questions that relate to what a candidate would do in a hypothetical situation that has been developed carefully as a means of testing a candidate's suitability for a role and an organization. A behavioral interview, of course, looks at a specific situation that has actually occurred in the past.

In my experience as a trainer and in my observations of successful organizations, I have found that while both approaches have high validity, the behavioral interview is a more practical system for

---

[4] Wiesner, 1–16.

a number of reasons. It allows interviewers to probe actual situations which are, consequently, filled with richer information than the situational interview yields.[5] It uses terms and events that have meaning for the people who are actually doing the work of the organization. And it does not come across as an academic system imposed by a team of psychologists, but rather as something that coheres and focuses what everyone already understands about their jobs and the organization's goals.

In my opinion, situational interviews are most useful in one key circumstance. When, after a series of behavioral interviews, you have reduced your pool of candidates to two or three indistinguishably suitable top performers, you can use a situational interview to pick the best candidate. The situation posed, however, should be related to an ethical issue currently alive within the organization. This is an invaluable means of determining how closely a candidate's personal values fit with the values of the organization.

The Odds and the Options

For a numerical comparison of the relative value of types of information gleaned from different interviewing approaches, let's look at some research. A meta-analytic study of 250 different interviewing processes done in the UK in 1989 came up with hard numbers to describe the prediction abilities of traditional and scientific approaches to interviewing.[6]

If you were to roll dice on a table in order to make your hiring decision, that choice would be totally random and would have zero validity. By looking at the educational level of the candidate, you give yourself a 10 percent chance of making a good choice. The résumé, on the other hand, provides for a 16 percent validity rate, while reference checks are higher still at 24 percent. The traditional one-on-one interview increases the likelihood of making the best hire to only 19 percent, which means that 81 percent of the information needed to make a good hiring decision is still missing in that

[5] Jeff A. Weekly and Joseph A.Gier "Reliability and Validity of the Situational Interview for a Sales Position," *Journal of Applied Psychology*, 72 No. 3, (1987): 484–487.
[6] Wiesner, 1–16.

most common of all methods. Meanwhile, traditional panel interviews, seen as a more stringent approach to selection, provide a 35 percent rate of validity. None of those numbers, it should be noted, are cumulative in their values. They are all stand-alone statistics.

If you use scientific approaches for making selection decisions, the odds are higher. Cognitive ability tests have a combined score of 54 percent with a 26 percent chance of good selection for routine jobs and a 69 percent chance for complex jobs. Work sample tests provide for 55 percent validity. Assessment centers, one of the most popular scientific methods of selection in today's corporate world, have a validity rate of 65 percent. Behavioral selection, on the other hand, has a validity rate of 70 percent.

Of scientific methods, the ones most worth comparing are assessment centers and the behavioral approach. A cost-benefit analysis of both, however, leads to an inescapable conclusion. Assessment centers require an enormous corporate investment— take from one to three days of a person's time, and yet do not match the validity rate of a behavioral interview. If I were the CFO of a company, I would choose to allocate my resources to the development of a behavioral system any time. In the real world, however, the best approach is not scientifically pure. The end goal is not to make a laboratory of the workplace but to meet the challenges of real-world employment markets head-on in order to get the best results. That is the guiding principle of this book, and it is reflected in the paths of the practitioners from the companies I profile throughout this book.

Determining the Economic Value-Added

Whether laying out the need for behavioral interviewing to the senior team or a line manager, calculating the economic value-added is sure to get their attention. To do so, analyze the situation your organization is in and plug in numbers that capture it in dollar terms. Beyond issues of accuracy, validity, and fairness, you will come up with compelling financial reasons to make the shift to a behavioral interview system. This is because both the direct and indirect costs of poor staffing decisions are enormous.

Direct costs of hiring include the search and interview process, training, benefits, salary, and so on. In general, depending on the level of the employee, most research estimates that the direct cost of a wrong hire is one to two-and-a-half times that employee's annual salary. For senior executives the cost ratio can increase to 10 times their annual salary. The impact of this on the organization's bottom line is easy to calculate. For instance, an engineering firm in Montreal had a 35 percent yearly turnover in its entry-level engineering positions. Since the average was not out of line with industry standards, the situation was considered acceptable given the strong employment market and the difficulty of attracting and keeping top talent. However, by developing a better hiring system that was more in tune with that organization's goals, values, and skill needs, turnover was reduced to seven percent annually. This saved the company millions of dollars from the get-go, and helped to pad those stock options and bonuses. Support for the initiative in that organization came, not surprisingly, from the CEO on down.

Indirect costs, though somewhat more difficult to calculate, are eye-opening nevertheless. Think of the losses in productivity, morale, and opportunity when employees are not a good fit for the organization or the role they are filling. What if your organization could function better, faster, and more effectively?

If you hire right, you gain cost savings right away, since those who are a better fit for the organization require less training and are more productive and effective at an earlier stage. Over the longer term, hiring people who fit the right values and behaviors of the company and achieve the desired business results, has a major positive impact on the business by providing improvements to such activities as production, customer service, and quality. If your organization has problems in these areas, it could be an indication of defective hiring or training. Analyze an under-performing division or area of your organization to test your ability to prove the need for better hiring or training practices. See if you find those links.

Few organizations look closely enough at what makes an employee fit their culture and thrive in it. The best have a vision and a goal of a more productive, innovative, and competitive workforce.

By providing a business argument for making an improvement in hiring practices, HR makes a strong contribution to the bottom line.

The following can be used as a model for how to define the cost of bad hiring. This analytical approach helps provide a sound business case for implantation of a behavioral hiring process.

Cost of Bad Hiring: A Bottom-Line Argument for Change

Current Hiring Process

1. Employee requisition
2. Internal posting (10-15 days)
3. External search (Agency costs 15 percent to 20 percent of annual salary 40K to 200K)
4. Find the top three candidates
5. HR screening
6. Pass along to hiring manager
7. Team follow-up interview
8. HR interview for fit to firm
9. Make offer for hire or continue the search process

The Problem

- Company's turnover is 25 percent (industry's is 15 percent)
- Objective is to reduce turnover to industry standard
- What is the cost of turnover?

The Logic

Based on an average starting salary of $75,000, the cost of an employee leaving within the first three years is calculated as follows:

Software Engineer Position

- These calculations are based on 10 open positions per year due to turnover
- Current type of recruiting strategy: Traditional Interviewing with validity factor of 0.19

- Direct recruiting costs: This represents the expenses of generating the applicant pool from which a selection will be made. It includes advertising, expenses in getting people the interviews, time people spend with candidates, time to check referrals, the cost to test candidates, and any assessment work done prior to hiring

- Number of applicants per opening (10 applications per opening)

- Percentage of offers accepted (if eight of 10 offers are accepted that would be 80 percent)

- Average salary: $75,000

- Average annual dollar spread in performance: This is a highly debated figure. It includes the cost of other people involved in training who are taken away from their roles. It also includes the cost of learning from mistakes. The acceptable average is 40 percent of base salary

- Number of shortlisted applicants per hire (range of three to five)

- Shortlist cost per applicant: Travel, use of facilities (cost of hotels), hiring managers' time (e.g. their salaries), and direct recruiting costs as listed above

- Screening cost per applicant: Cost includes the time spent opening and reviewing resumes, calling applicants, arranging the interviews internally, and making travel arrangements

- Selection screening information: Such as assessment centers; if cost is nothing, then zero

- Cost of legal fees (internal or external) for the hiring contract and for severance

Once the above costs are determined, the calculation can be estimated. Based on the research already completed at other organizations, we know that for entry-level positions that turn within the first year, the cost of hiring is 1.5 times salary, while the executive cost per individual is 10 times the salary.

The average annual dollar spread is a difficult calculation because it includes lost opportunity cost. If your employee takes a client with him or her to a new firm, or has learned a process or idea that they can be used to the advantage of a competitor, there is a significant lost opportunity cost. The calculation, however, is difficult, if not impossible, to determine in advance and will vary by incident.

Other Factors to Consider

The cost of hiring the wrong person and the chances of improving the hiring decision are a matter of taking a process that is currently accurate at the level of 0.19 accuracy and moving it to an accuracy level of 0.70. The increase is 2.6 times more efficient. What does this mean in real dollars?

If you interview for 10 openings:

- You consider three people per opening
- You have to interview 30 people
- You have to consider reviewing at least 90 résumés
- You have to interview the final candidates four times
- You pay $15,000 per hire to a search firm for 10 positions for $150,000
- You take 40 percent of salary for performance spread for cost to train within the first year for $30,000
- The cost of one ad in a national newspaper for $15,000
- The cost of the interview process for each person interviewing with HR, hiring managers, and for team members and HR again (excluding travel and related expenses) is about $4,500 per applicant
- You take lost opportunity cost at 40 percent for a software engineer when he or she moves on to the competition at $30,000 per hire
- Cost of severance and associated legal costs: $5,000

- Cost of annual salary for a full one year before an employee leaves: $75,000

- Cost of a person leaving within the first three years: $175,000

Conclusion: The Bottom Line

If you were to lose 25 percent of your employees and that represents 25 employees per year, the cost per year would be $4,312,500 per year for bad hiring decisions. If you change from traditional interviewing (accuracy of 0.19) to behavioral interviewing (accuracy 0.70) you can reduce that by half and save $2,156,250 annually.

Getting Buy-In From the Organization

Securing ongoing organizational support for a behavioral interviewing system can be a challenge. As with any significant effort, an intervention into hiring will require time, resources, and commitment from a wide cross section of people. If you are the champion driving this effort, your perseverance, determination, and agility will be tested along with your business partnering and selling skills. You will need a solid strategy for gaining buy-in that's suited to the particular needs of your organization and that can be adjusted, depending on the stage of your implementation.

In some organizations, the mandate for change comes from the top down; in others, employees and line managers are often ahead of the curve and see the desperate need for change before senior management does. No matter where your base comes from, selling is one of the prime skills you will need every step of the way. You will have to use arguments that make sense to whomever you are trying to convince. With senior or line management, this might mean breaking down the numbers to present the business case and the economic value-added. With employees, you may find it more helpful to clarify how behavioral profiles connect the actual work of the job to rewards and recognition.

In *Chapter 3: The Organization, the Job, and the Candidate: The Right Fit*, we will introduce two case studies, one from Michelin North America and the other from Sprint Canada. The Michelin North America approach began their journey on behavioral interviewing with entry-level engineers. The Sprint Canada journey began with a commitment from the senior executive team. Both paths lead to the process eventually being adopted corporately.

No matter what path you take, you will develop supporters and fellow champions along the way. All converts have a positive effect on those around them. Still, remember to keep them on track. Sometimes people will believe you wholeheartedly but forget all of the important steps required, or they won't fully understand what it takes to achieve the results you want in the interview.

Case Studies: Two Approaches to Behavioral Interviewing

As with any organizational effectiveness intervention, when it comes to implementing a behavioral interviewing system, two traditional approaches exist. You can either use a blanket approach, developing a system that encompasses the hiring practices of the entire organization, or you can use an opportunity-driven approach by working with a single department or manager involved with some business imperative and then exhibiting those results to the rest of the organization. To better understand these two approaches, consider the following real-life cases.

Abbott Labs

Abbott Labs took an opportunity-driven approach by targeting the leaders of strategic change initiatives. "Some organizations are very corporate, elaborate, and top-down driven," Andrée Charbonneau points out. "At Abbot—a very large company—it can be difficult to get everyone doing something at the same time. The champion approach can therefore be very effective. You zero in on people who really need what you're trying to show and use them as champions."

It was not difficult to convince someone initiating a strategic plan of the need to improve the accuracy of hiring decisions. "What is really helpful," Andrée says, "is that we are on the client system here so that I spend most of my time with my customers in the pharmaceutical products division and go to all their business meetings." Working together through strategy issues made it easier to suggest a retooling of the hiring system and gave it what it needed—a behavioral focus more grounded in the work of the organization than the off-the-shelf system had provided.

After the success of several trials, Andrée found that people started talking about the results and the experience. As one manager said, "My God, after those interviews I really felt that I knew those candidates. And now that I've selected someone, I have confidence that they're good." Soon after, other managers called and asked how they too could begin to do behavioral profiles. The results spoke for themselves and the technique spread.

"It can be a very daunting task for an organization to say, 'we're going to change our approach to interviewing and in order to do that we have to develop competency profiles for all jobs,' particularly if the company is changing very rapidly." Working with business managers most in need of making new hires, HR at Abbott Labs worked with divisions that were restructuring and developed competency profiles needed for the change to be successful. "It helps," Andrée says, "to have a senior HR person involved driving the initiative—someone who understands and can react to business issues as they surface, and who knows the organization well enough to coordinate forces with the appropriate people."

Calgary Police Service

Rather than moving from division to division, the top-down approach was used at the Calgary Police Service, a solution perhaps best suited to its hierarchical structure and paramilitary culture. The seed was planted by the new Chief of Police, Christine Silverberg, when she conducted an appraisal of issues that concerned the organization and quickly determined that there was widespread dissatisfaction with the promotion process. The introduction of a behavioral competency approach made sense but, despite the call for change, getting the rank and file to accept a new set of goals and success measurements was not easy or without risk.

I asked Inspector Dale Burns what it was like being a champion for this initiative. His answer was forthright and typical of other people's experiences.

"Brutal. You have to realize that it's a total change of culture. Here's me, this jerk from HR, saying our promotional process is changing. Organizational buy-in is particularly important here. You've got a paramilitary organization that's been around a hundred years, has a machismo attitude, and this is a softer approach."

Selling the organizational base was a full-time job. "I attended every parade, every team day. They're sick of me. But when we get someone in each area to have some knowledge and be fired into this, they sell it to their 20 sergeants and they sell it to the constables and each year it's getting better. The knowledge in lower levels has gone a long way."

Beyond ongoing persistence, the ultimate issue Dale found was getting people to agree philosophically with the new approach. "The key to getting them to listen was that they actually believe in it because it makes sense." Using focus groups helped. When the people doing the work of policing were called upon to "articulate the values and competencies [by themselves and in their own words] they actually came up with *customer service, focus, compassion*; it was nice to hear that from the grassroots." But before the focus groups, those behaviors had never thrived as well as they should because they weren't defined clearly and they weren't supported. The new system does that.

Sprint Canada

Sprint Canada also used a top-down approach but the idea for the initiative was sold to senior management who then embraced it and made it an operating principle.

After calculating the cost savings and the strategic advantages of using a behavioral interviewing system, HR gained respect from the senior executive team by openly acknowledging the issues that the organization was facing and speaking up about the business need for changing its hiring practices. Declaring that there was a problem with recruitment and retention, HR impressed upon the CEO the costs involved, statistically proving that Sprint was losing $3 million to $4 million a year through poor retention without even calculating losses in opportunity, customer satisfaction levels, and speed-to-market. "It's essential to be supported from the top," Victoria Walker, vice president of human resources, says, "otherwise it's all show and it's not really working."

With the go-ahead, HR took a snapshot in time of the status quo and developed a profile of what the organization needed to do in the future. Looking at existing star performers, HR helped to identify the successful behaviors of employees today and what they thought would be the predictors of success in the markets of tomorrow. Firmly linking its approach to the core values of the organization as a market-driven enterprise, HR increased its synergy and working relationship with the marketing department and translated all of its behavioral terms into market language—a key to selling it internally.

Getting commitment for behavioral profiles from the employees themselves was not difficult. Victoria found that focus groups helped dramatically with buy-in. "People wanted to do focus groups. They were very involved in it and really owned the process. Because the language so related to the work, they really saw that it was going to happen. It hit home more than we expected. A lot of times you put these initiatives out and you really have to coax people, but we didn't. Everybody was very, very into it right from top to bottom."

She admits that, like anything, it needs a champion to keep going. But "the good thing is people asked for it. They would say, 'I'm doing this [new business] now and I have this whole new group of employees and I don't have a success profile or I don't have an interview guide,' and we would hear this every time the hiring manager needed help, and that tells me that they're using it."

Victoria's take on the benefits of tackling this initiative across Sprint Canada at one time is clear. "Our company at the time was small enough to do it across the board, and we didn't have any existing processes in place—it was a clean slate. That made it probably one of the easiest implementations from that point of view: we weren't breaking down an old system; we were putting in something that didn't exist. Anything would be great."

Victoria recognizes, however, that a solution must be geared to the particular needs of each organization. "It depends on your current situation. You could put this in place in a semi-autonomous work unit where you had a fair degree of 'we're on our own,' or a division that's fairly autonomous. But it's where you start to cross paths, and employees don't stay in one place. That's the biggest impact and concern. If employees don't see consistency, and if they can't talk the same language across the company, it starts to create problems.

"It's a great great tool for any company, but especially for a company that gets to a certain size and realizes, okay, now we have to put in structure, because you can do it right from the get-go."

HMV Canada

Marnie Falkiner has learned that it helps to speak in the language of the people you need to convince. Though in human resources at HMV Canada at the time, Marnie has an operations background and knew what buttons to push with regional managers. That understanding gave her an edge in gaining support for a behavioral system from the field. "Measuring things gives credibility. It proves the business need. And you measure the changes when you implement something [to continue support for that intervention]."

As already detailed, Marnie analyzed the profitability issues that resulted from a lack of training and high turnover in order to make her argument. Once she implemented behavioral profiles, she tracked those improvements in order to show the positive impact. This helped because senior management "still struggles with the behavioral part of it and the value of that. They're afraid of it. What they don't like about HR is all that intangible stuff and intuition and so on."

Positive feedback from the operations VP and the regional managers continued the momentum. "They were quite involved, felt a part of it and had strong ownership. Coming out of operations, it wasn't difficult to be able to talk with them."

And feedback and support from ground level employees was also strong. "A lot of these people felt that they were getting the best business education that they'd ever had, and it was the first time they had been treated as adults. They had tattoos and rings in their noses and you wanted to call their parents and say, 'do you know how responsible your child is? Do you know she's running a $4 million business and doing great?' So there was a lot of pride in themselves that they were learning."

But Marnie is not hesitant to talk about the challenges as well. "The hardest part is to get the buy-in from senior management. I went to it almost indirectly. I was there to look at a financial problem. You need to find a way to sell this to an organization so that they actually see the value of it from sort of an ROI point of view. Everyone wants to be nice. Everyone thinks they do treat everyone nice. But getting into this behavioral stuff is probably the hardest thing for them to understand. You kind of get lip-service. 'Yeah, we'll let you do it.' And you sort of get some dollars. You need to find a way to define success to bring it back to the organization quickly so that they keep supporting you and let you do it. Otherwise the project gets stuck. You either lose resources to be able to do it or lose funds to be able to continue. And if you don't go through it quickly to get something out there, you have a problem. And if you don't involve the people enough, then it loses credibility too."

Once it got off the ground, however, the issue of support was a different matter. "Management didn't have a chance because it was being driven now by the employees—wanted by the employees. If you don't get that kind of buy-in early, then you struggle with trying to keep it alive."

Thomas Cook

Christine Deputy has had it both ways. At Thomas Cook the intervention was top-down and implemented across the entire division. Accompanied by a customer service initiative, behavioral interviewing made strategic sense and also had the backing of a senior executive involved not just in HR but overall business strategy. She worked closely with this finance-oriented manager, bringing her people knowledge into the equation, and was trusted to do whatever she needed in a very decentralized environment. As was true when she went to the top, internally there was almost no sell required.

Starbucks

At Starbucks Christine had to introduce behavioral interviewing into a very different culture. "It was a fun challenge because it's not a process-oriented company at all. But it's an organization that, when it sees value in doing something, buys in." As she describes it, "It took me about four months to get the support to try this, and the other day I had a conversation with the director of training who said to me, 'Christine, we can't do it any other way. You've made a believer of me.'"

She found that adjusting for different circumstances makes behavioral interviewing valuable no matter the corporate cultures. "You can modify it for different environments. It's flexible enough and can give you a product that is robust enough to live in an environment that is very fast-paced as well."

The difficulty now is in being the only real knowledgeable champion of the system at the senior level while still dealing with the fast pace of a company that always wants to move on to the next challenge. Developing concrete outputs like career products and establishing financial impact helps. "There's a big time commitment. That's probably the biggest challenge from an organizational standpoint. If we get our recruiters skilled up and if they help others build some zealots, it's worth it. The payoff's huge. When you hire wrong, it's too expensive. If you've hired them and they only stay six months, it costs a year's salary. If you get a bunch of bad hires in your organization, your business is going to suffer. When you get turnover at the hourly level, you lose customer intimacy; you lose the spirit of what we're doing."

Summary

In today's economic climate, hiring the best people is crucial to staying competitive. Traditional interviewing methods, with their emphasis on such tools as the résumé, references, and lists of experience, fail to capture the complexity of figuring out who is really right for the job. Behavioral interviewing offers an alternative and behavior-oriented approach. Much more than a system of interviewing, it's a total commitment to change in how an organization conceives and presents itself both internally and externally. As such, behavioral interviewing requires people with vision and passion to sell it within the organization. But as the case studies so clearly show, the commitment and hard work pays off. In the next chapter, we'll look at how to define "the right fit."

⬙⬙

CHAPTER 3

The Organization, the Job, and the Candidate: The Right Fit

Understanding What To Look For

Whether we are talking about behavioral, situational, or traditional interviews, selection decisions fail for one of two reasons: either we don't know what we are looking for or we don't know how to assess what we have learned.

In this chapter we will discuss the parameters for determining what it is we should be examining when interviewing candidates. Though nothing could be more important, too often this basic consideration is taken for granted. We must, however, be deliberate about what questions we ask and what parameters we use in determining the suitability of a candidate, since we are likely to learn only that which we are trying to understand. As any scientist will confirm, you can only expect to get results from the data that you inspect.

Just as important, if we hire based on a correct notion of what is needed in the organization, we reinforce our alignment of strategy and people. On the other hand, if we hire incorrectly, we throw yet another wrench into any chance we have of truly organizing our workforce to achieve our strategic goals.

Employee Success and Failure

Based on exit interviews, we found that 87 percent of those who leave an organization or fail in a role, do so not because of their skills—the reason they were originally hired—but because of their behavior—the way they performed on the job.[1] This hard data backs up a general observation about success and failure for employees within organizations. No matter what industry, people are hired for their technical knowledge, promoted for their innovation, and fired for their behavior.

When making a hiring decision, we determine whether a candidate fits the bill by examining their technical knowledge—their academic or training background and past work experience. In spite of this, once on the job, we identify success with innovation. In other words, we do not promote those who perform at average levels, who merely accomplish what they are supposed to do. In fact, we value those who create improvements, prompt positive change, and impact the bottom line in an exceptional way. Finally, whenever we are forced to fire an employee, it is always related to his or her behaviors—how he or she perform on the job, and manages him- or herself interpersonally, his or her approach, orientation to time or detail, and level of assertiveness or risk. All of these things confirm whether an employee fits into the organization's culture, goals, expectations, and ways of doing things.

In keeping with the causes for failure, research also confirms that organizational fit is a key factor in retaining the best employees. The McKinsey-Sibson report, "The War for Talent"[2] examines why high-tech employees choose to leave or stay with an organization. The technology sector is a particularly appropriate industry to look at because employment markets prior to early 2001 were so

---

[1] David Cohen, 1988, unpublished.
[2] McKinsey-Sibson, *The War for Talent: Building a Superior Talent Pool to Drive Company Performance* (McKinsey & Company, 1997–2000).

hot that workers were more or less free to determine their own fates. If they wished to stay in an organization, low unemployment rates made it unlikely they would be fired under any circumstances; if they wished to jump ship, another employment opportunity could easily be secured. Under these circumstances, what motivates a decision to stay or go is highly indicative of what all employees look for in an organization.

The findings are fascinating. In the high pay-off world of dot-coms, initial public offerings, and stock options, money ranked 13 out of 20 for reasons a high-tech employee would choose to leave an organization. As any manager knows, it's very easy for an employee who's jumping ship to tell you that he or she has gotten a better offer somewhere else. As the study shows, although this may be the easiest explanation, the real reason probably isn't expressed.

The opportunity to travel ranked fourth on the list. Apparently, for young people already devoting much of their youth to their career, the possibility of combining work with a chance to see the world is a tremendous draw.

Third on the list of reasons for leaving were development opportunities—namely, was there sufficient learning on the job and enough opportunities to play with the latest and greatest technological toys?

The top two reasons on the list relate directly to the central argument of this book. The second stated reason for leaving was whether people felt they would have opportunities for meaningful professional and or personal development. The number one reason was the lack of cultural fit—misalignment between the individual's values and the actual values demonstrated daily by the company.

The Importance of Defining Fit

The best fit occurs when a person's capabilities—the combination of his or her skills, knowledge, and behaviors—matches the job's requirements and the organization's culture.

When the fit is strong, outstanding performance and job satisfaction are the result. It can be measured indirectly in terms of productivity and levels of innovation and directly in rates of retention.

While it is true that the best way to predict future performance is to analyze a candidate's past behavior, that is only half of the equation. You must consider your corporate culture, values, and the related behaviors required on the job—*before* you start the process. No matter how good the interview or how probing and insightful the questions, your interview is not going to be as effective as it should be without first defining fit.

When *fit* is not defined, the organization typically ends up comparing one candidate to another. The result, of course, is that the "best" candidate is decided on in comparison to the other applicants. Determining fit in advance allows you to consider each candidate in the light of what the organization needs. When this is done, you might discover that none of the candidates you are currently interviewing are a good match for the position, despite their appealing attributes, personality, or background. The best, most economically and organizationally sound business decision in such a case is to continue the search. To do otherwise is to waste time, money, and yet another opportunity to improve organizational effectiveness.

Organizational Values

Every organization has a set of values, whether it is explicitly acknowledged or operating below the surface like a hidden curriculum. As a definition, *values* are strongly held beliefs that are emotionally charged, highly resistant to change, and long-standing. They are the genetic thread that encodes an organization's instincts and philosophy and the source of its culture, strategy, and work styles.

Are they real? Think of any great organization, one whose members truly live its values, and you will see the power of a coherent set of beliefs, fought for, adhered to, and used as a guiding set of principles. There are plenty of examples within the business world. *Built to Last*,[3] by Jim Collins and Jerry Porras describes the

---

[3] James C. Collins and Jerry I. Porras, *Built to Last* (New York: Harper Business, 1994).

likes of GE, Disney, Hewlett-Packard, and so on, almost exclusively as organizations that developed into their current manifestations based on a core set of beliefs and a long-term vision. Think of the "HP Way" or Disney's explicit purpose to "bring happiness to millions" while operating in accordance with family values. Notice how their employees over generations have held to such a philosophy and way of doing work.

As an example outside today's business world, consider the British Empire. It was run with only six layers of hierarchy, from Queen to common foot soldier. Yet the value set of that organization (upon which the sun never set for hundreds of years) was so clear that any member of it was able to run any aspect of it from anywhere in the world without question or hesitation.

Not all organizations are so explicit about their values and reasons for being. They are, however, poorer for it. If values are not already explicit, concrete, understood by everyone, and hence alive within the organization, a consensus should be developed as to what they are—before beginning the development of a behavioral interviewing system. If values are already a part of your organization, then they can be used to check against and confirm the rightness of your job profiles when they have been defined and written.

When clearly articulated, values provide a road map for success because they are the source for every action or decision made by members of that organization. Indeed, values determine how the organization defines success and how it builds its talent pool, when and under what circumstances people are recognized, rewarded, or let go, and how people are developed and promoted. Their influence on every aspect of an organization and its employees cannot be overstated. When employees who fit with the organization's values are hired, they reinforce those values and align with the organization's vision, strategy, and best-work practices.

When, on the other hand, values exist but are unconnected to how the organization really works, rewards and, of course, hires, a poisonous and harmful disconnect is fostered. I'm sure we all have had this experience. You join a new company and the first thing you do is try to figure out what your boss, the department, and the organization as a whole really expects. And where does that information come from? This essential information is rarely learned by reading the policy manual or the corporate mission, attending the orientation session, or during the interview itself; instead, it is sought out and discovered during lunch breaks, in line-ups at the fax machine, and impromptu conversations with co-workers over coffee or before meetings. Bit by bit we determine the rules, the things that we must do to be successful. We soon learn to tune out or mock what upper management proclaims and to act on what it really rewards.

Values must be real. They cannot be just words on a business card or a corporate home page. They must be articulated behaviorally, celebrated when demonstrated, and corrected when violated. Otherwise, you are making a powerful message to your new recruits: this organization is confused and you are bound for frustration, stress, and a lack of clarity about what you should do to be a top performer. Here are some examples of clearly articulated core values from the organizations that practice behavioral interviewing.

Thomas Cook

OUR MISSION

To create the best and most profitable travel-driven service business in the world.

OUR VALUES

Working For Thomas Cook Means:

- Taking Personal Responsibility for Achieving the Mission

- Pursuing Excellence in Everything We Do

- Displaying Honesty and Trust in all Our Relations with Customers, Colleagues, Business Partners, Shareholders and Striving to Deliver Outstanding Service to Them at all Times

- Recognising and Respecting the Needs of Individuals

HMV Core Values

HMV is committed to providing a great work environment and satisfying jobs for all employees. The following core values outline the way we believe our staff and customers should be treated:

- People are mature adults and deserve dignity
- People want to work hard and obtain substantial fulfillment from their work
- People want to be committed to the company and achieve personal fulfillment from this commitment
- Performance achievement goals should always be a stretch- but they should never be unachievable
- People can and should be trusted
- People want to belong to a high-performance company
- People perform better if they have:

  Voice: a say in what affects their work
  Autonomy: the ability to contribute and add value
  Understanding: of the company's vision, values, and objectives
  Security/Reward: commitment is two-way
  Development: opportunities to develop and utilize their skills

Sprint Canada Values

TEAMWORK–Fostering a collaborative working environment where people actively share information, rely on each other's expertise, deliver on commitments, and trust each other.

- Shares the credit and success with team by celebrating together
- Puts the organization and teams goals above own personal agenda

RESPONSIVENESS–Responding quickly to requests of internal and external customers, providing realistic commitments to manage the expectations of others, taking ownership to get things done.

- Provides others help in a prompt and timely manner when requested
- States honestly what can be done and by when, thus managing expectations of others

INNOVATION–Generating and implementing creative solutions. Trying different and novel ways in dealing with change and opportunity.

- Frequently asks for the involvement of others in solving problems
- Tolerates trying, failing, and learning, celebrating together when learning leads to improvements

BALANCE–Recognizing the need for a lifestyle that reflects balance for the individual, contributing towards a positive work environment, valuing and being sensitive to individual differences.

- Proactively manages career by seeking new information and learning experiences
- Finds things to laugh about and openly has fun to help reduce tension or stress

For management, the responsibilities go even deeper than good hiring and clear performance management. When it comes to the long-term steering of the organization, values must never be compromised, even in the face of competition or an opportunity to enhance the bottom line. They define the essence of the corporate soul. If you violate them, you will pay the price for years to come. If you hold them true, you will make the right business decisions no matter what curves innovation, new markets, competition, or unforeseen bumps in the road throw your way. Ask Johnson & Johnson what it was like when the Tylenol scare took place. Compare that to the way Firestone handled its recent problems.

Organizational Culture

The culture of an organization is a pattern of basic assumptions invented, discovered, or developed by the group as it learns to cope with situations. Such assumptions are validated through practice and passed on or taught to new employees as the correct way to perceive, feel, think, and act in relation to the work of the organization. While values are set by the people who lead organizations, culture is a form of group consensus in relation to those values, developing in the dark, as it were, when no one's paying attention.

You can easily measure the effectiveness of your link between values and your hiring practices by looking at corporate culture. Does it reflect your organization's values? Does it work every day to implement those values behaviorally? When a gap exists, your organization's people systems are out of line. You are hiring, promoting, recognizing, rewarding, and disciplining in conflict with your own organizational reason for being. On the other hand, alignment of culture and values with the way employees are recruited, managed, promoted, and fired creates tremendous organizational power.

Organizational Vision

Corporate vision, too, emerges from an organization's values. A "vision" is a desired future state, the core of strategic thinking that needs to precede strategic planning. It is something that motivates and excites employees and makes them want to belong, and it is about why you exist as a company. A vision is never fully attained; it represents something worthwhile and significant always to be strived for.

Correctness of vision has to be measured against values, not the other way round. Many companies make the mistake of articulating vision first and then deciding on the values necessary to achieve that vision. The central reason to exist rings hollow and creates distress if not backed up by organizational values that employees understand, believe in, and use as a guiding principle. People work for a sense of impact and belonging and a chance to achieve a vision, not simply for a paycheck.

Corporate Mission, Strategy, and Objectives

Business strategy or corporate mission, on the other hand, is the road map in the short run to achieve long-term vision. While mission or strategy will change from year to year, depending on markets, customers, technology, and opportunity, a vision statement based on values stays the same no matter what the economic circumstances. With strategy or mission, the business case and the people case come together.

In order to achieve a major corporate goal, the organization needs to hire, train, and reward employees in alignment with its short-term objectives, medium-term mission, and long-term vision, all based ultimately on its core values.

Linking Values to Behaviors

The diagram on the following page illustrates the alignment and continuum between organizational values and individual work styles or behaviors.

The reality of the link between values and behaviour was illustrated dramatically for me recently. I was involved in developing behavior profiles for customer service representatives at three different banks in the same market. With mortgage rates so low that there is no financial advantage in going to one bank over another, the differentiating factor for customers is the way the organization's values are expressed in its corporate image and in the lasting impression of the behaviors exhibited by the customer service reps.

As if to highlight how clearly values affect strategy, training, and hiring, I was fascinated by the profound differences among those

Consistency Between Word and Action

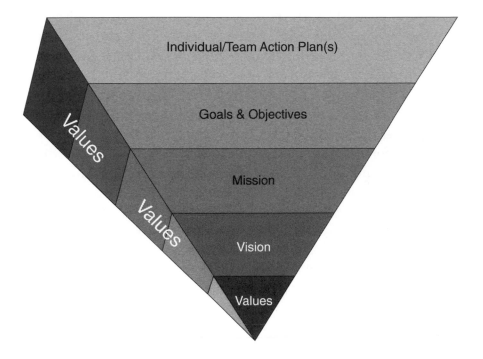

© Strategic Action Group, Ltd.

three customer service representative profiles. One bank is focused on building a learning organization and another is focused on developing its people. A third bank is aiming for a retail approach and yet a fourth in the same market is honing in on thoroughness and efficiency. Naturally, the behaviors required by a customer service rep in each organization reflect that bank's overall vision. An employee who is a top performer in one organization cannot be transferred readily into another, because the behaviors required are different.

And yet, for most organizations, information about their values and the corresponding behavior is only rarely included in the job description. When behaviors and values are explicitly described in the job profile, you have a chance to attract and identify the right people.

The What and How of a Job

On the other side of the fit equation is the individual employee. Every employee brings his or her capabilities to a job. When we talk about a person's knowledge, skills, and behaviors, we are referring to his or her own individual mix of expertise and technical know-how, as well as the way they go about doing a job. As we've already shown, technical know-how is thoroughly examined in traditional interviews. Behaviors, on the other hand, are touched on only incidentally or not at all, even though they are the determining factor in whether a candidate will fit an organization and thus succeed or fail.

Another way of thinking about this is to break down the "what" and "how"—"what" is done on the job and "how" one is expected to do it.

The "what" of a job focuses on the skills and knowledge required in a role and is defined in terms of tasks and objectives. Some of the determining parameters are the job description itself— organizational policies and standard procedures, the responsibilities of the role, and the physical methods used to get the work done—in other words, traditional job description statements.

The "how" of a job involves the behaviors required to perform a job's roles successfully. Those behaviors move beyond the requirements of the position itself to the context of the organization at large. The "how" of a job is defined implicitly by the organization's true values and the organization's management principles such as team norms, work relationships, and the organizational culture.

Successful performers are distinguished by "how" they behave in the workplace to achieve desired business results. The achievement of results alone is not enough. We all know that bottom-line thinking can view any behavior or work method as acceptable "if it gets results." This is fine in the short run, but in the long run, obtaining results in the wrong ways creates collateral damage to which no organization is immune. By recognizing and rewarding results that are obtained in the wrong way, an organization is sending a significant message to its employees, and probably to its customers, about its lack of adherence to its own stated values and operating principles.

Besides, when results are achieved in the wrong ways, we might be very wrong about their actual benefits. A loan officer I observed had the best numbers in her division. This was thought to be because of, rather than in spite of, her cut-throat nature. When, after a serious interpersonal issue she was reluctantly let go, numbers for the division as a whole rose more than enough to make up for her loss. Undoubtedly her ways of doing business were interfering with the performance of her colleagues and, perhaps ultimately, of the organization.

Daniel Goleman, the author of *Emotional Intelligence in the Workplace*, a recent study of successful performance in different job categories, had this to say about computer programmers:

> ...the top 10 percent of computer programmers exceed average performers in producing effective programs by 320 percent. And the top 1 percent of programmers produce a mind-boggling 1,272 percent more than the average. The deciding factors: a willingness to collaborate, not compete; to stay late to help others; to share shortcuts.[4]

In other words, if we believe that it is acceptable for computer programmers to be antisocial and even hostile to their fellow employees because it is in their nature, we might allow for behaviors that are actually significant factors in under-performance as measured by the bottom line. If, on the other hand, we know that in the context of our organization the most significant indicator of productivity as a computer programmer is not technical ability, speed, innovation, or academic background but cooperative behavior, we have dramatically increased our ability to identify and select top performers from the candidate pool and enable ourselves to reward and reinforce the right behaviors in our current employees.

---

[4] Daniel Goleman, *Emotional Intelligence in the Workplace* (New York: Harper Business, 1994).

Technical Knock-Out Factors

A caution needs to be applied here, however, when considering the "what" and "how" of a job. In their eagerness to embrace behavioral interviews, some people swing too far in the other direction and overlook technical skills and knowledge. Perhaps the following formula will help strike the right balance.

$$C = (S + K) \times B$$

In other words, the *capabilities* of a person is a function of their *skills* plus their *knowledge* multiplied by their *behaviors*.

Traditional interviews focus on skills and knowledge. Behavioral interviews focus on behaviors. Behaviors, as can be seen in the formula, are a more significant aspect of overall success, but they are not the only factor in the equation.

If we hire only for organizational fit, we may find that the candidate is unable to do the job at the necessary level of sophistication. So we should not forget about testing for skills and knowledge. I would recommend the following: since it's easier to test for skills and knowledge, consider them your knock-out factors for the job. Through an examination of credentials, resume, educational level and required tests, you should ensure that a candidate has those knock-out factors before proceeding to the behavioral interview.

Can-Do and Will-Do Factors

To get a better grasp of how behaviors and behavioral tendencies function in the complex personality of an individual, picture an onion. An onion is easy to peel on the surface, but it has many layers. The top layer represents a person's skills and knowledge. The top layer is easy to observe, easy for an individual to exhibit or demonstrate, but is highly changeable depending on circumstances and conditions. As a means of predicting success, the top layer has little impact on future performance.

At a slightly deeper layer, but still close to the surface, are the "can-do" factors that indicate a person's background and experience. As interviewers, we need to make more direct inquiries to reach this level of observation. But this layer still doesn't tell us how the candidate will apply his or her experiences on the job.

Beneath these layers, at the core of the onion, are the "will-do" factors that drive actual behavior. Because will-do factors are stable and less subject to change, they are key when it comes to selection of the right candidate. They tell us the extent to which someone *will* use their knowledge and skills on the job and *how* he or she will do so.

Behavioral Competencies

Will-do factors are what people mean when they refer to behaviors or behavioral competencies. Whether someone will actually exhibit a behavior is not so much a function of ability as it is of motives and values—the essential piece of information required to understand a person's capabilities.

Behavioral competencies have been around for some time now. They were first identified in 1941 by the U.S. Air Force and U.S. Navy in their studies of what made one fighter pilot more effective than another. In their research, the U.S. Air Force and U.S. Navy aimed to determine whether training, background, physical or mental attributes, or some combination of these created a better pilot. Ultimately, it was determined that behavior rather than technical knowledge was the differentiating factor. This line of research was quickly picked up by businesses as a useful methodology. In 1949, research was conducted at a Delco battery plant in Dearborn, Michigan, to define the basic conditions necessary for employees to be successful and effective. The work done in that research evolved into the first assessment center.[5]

---

[5] John C. Flanagan. (1947) The aviation psychology program in the Army Air Forces. Washington: U.S. Government Printing Office, (*AAF Aviat, Psychol. Program Res. Rep. No. 1*) & Milner, N.E. (1947) Psychological researach on pilot training. Washington: U.S. Government Printing Office (*AAF Aviat Psychol. Program Res. Rep. No. 8*)

Other terms for "behaviors" are also used. The most common term in North America is "competencies," in the UK "competence." Practitioners often like to use a term more in accordance with achievement such as "success factors" or "performance dimensions." I prefer "behavior" or "behavioral competency" because it emphasizes action or doing rather than an innate quality or result. We are, after all, interested in what people actually do on the job, and it's helpful to keep that front and center in the terms we use.

Despite the variation in terminology, people agree that we are all focusing on the same thing—what outstanding performers do that distinguishes them from average or poor performers. My personal definition of a behavioral competency is: "the smallest unit of on-the-job behavior that is observable, measurable, and subject to change or improvement over time." The Hay/McBer definition is "any motive, attitude, skill, knowledge, behavior, or other personal (underlying) characteristic that is essential to perform the job or differentiates the average from the superior performer."[6]

Jobs typically require a cluster of behavioral competencies. Job fit, again, is a function of how much that competency cluster is overlapped by the behavioral competencies of the individual along with his or her technical skills and knowledge. Not everyone working in a role or job family will have the same set of competencies, but competencies can be developed or improved since they are subject to change. The important thing is to go for maximum fit and train the rest, keeping in mind that all development, and indeed, selection of behavioral competencies must be done in the proper context. In other words, to be useful, behavioral competencies must be critical to the success of what the organization wants to accomplish in its strategic business plan. Without that link, behavioral competencies are not a worthwhile contribution, even though they do make a person nicer, more interesting, more well-rounded, less cynical, or a better joke teller.

---

[6] Lyle M. Spencer and Signe Spencer. *Competence at Work: Models for Superior Performance*—1 edition, (1993).

Transferability: The Hierarchy of Behaviors

Unlike skills or knowledge, a behavioral competency is intrinsic to a person, an underlying characteristic that is consistently displayed. It is transferable, meaning that a behavioral competency exhibited in one circumstance will be exhibited in other circumstances as well. Linked to deeply set values, motives, and intents, behavioral competencies are intrinsically bound to the individual.

This concept of transferability is the key theoretical basis for the usefulness of behavioral interviews. When looking for examples of behavior typical of what is needed in a position, you do not require a perfect match between the circumstances of the role and the previous circumstances in which the individual exhibited that behavior. Rather, keep in mind the hierarchy of behaviors:

- The more recent the past behavior, the more likely it is to be repeated
- The more often the behavior was demonstrated over time, the higher the probability it will be repeated in the future

If directly related experiences are not available for probing, then probing for transferable behaviors is a statistically valid way to make selection decisions.

The concept of transferable behaviors brings great relief to my son, a recent college graduate, and it should bring equal relief to hiring managers looking for candidates who are capable of moving into new roles in our ever-evolving economy. My son and many young people like him are often worried about being caught in the catch-22 of no chance of employment without prior experience; in other words, they fear no one will hire them without experience while at the same time it is impossible to gain experience without first being hired. Recruiters, on the other hand, fear that in a competitive employment market or for roles that are new in the organization, it is difficult to identify and select the best, since the pool of top candidates, as measured by direct experience, can be small. Take the following example. A woman, recently graduated with her masters in library science, was preparing to enter the job market. As a stay-at-home mom who had not been in the workforce for the last 16 years, she felt that she lacked relevant job experience. As a result, she was considerably worried about her ability to compete with other candidates, many of whom were barely older than her oldest daughter.

A profile of the job she applied for (librarian at a large, urban hospital) focused on key competencies like "anticipating and satisfying diverse needs," "multi-tasking," "organizational discipline, *and* flexibility." Despite her lack of direct work experience, the behaviors she had exhibited in being the mother of three active girls while excelling in a demanding academic field, made her, in fact, a perfect candidate for the job. This was revealed through the interview and she was selected on the spot, over younger candidates who were also fresh out of school but could not demonstrate any such real-life examples of the desired behaviors.

David Campbell of the Center for Creative Leadership tells a great anecdote which illustrates this point well. Two senior managers are discussing one particularly successful, top-performing junior employee named Ben. Manager A says, "Ben really enjoys his job and that's why he's the best damn worker I've ever had and that's why I'm going to keep him happy." Manager B disagrees and counters: "No, Ben likes his job because he does it so well. To keep him happy and keep him on board you should do whatever it takes to further improve his performance." In speeches, David Campbell asks "Who is right in their assessment of why Ben is happy, Manager A or Manager B?

The answer is Manager A. As Campbell says, "find a happy junior employee, and you will find a happy executive years down the road." This is because happiness or optimism, perseverance, perfectionism, cynicism, defensiveness, or any other intrinsic trait or competency goes deeper than external circumstances. Arising from an internal source, such characteristics are predominantly exhibited in a person's behavior no matter what situation they find themselves in.

Given the choice between an untrained person with the right behaviors and values coupled with the untested knowledge to do most of the job, or someone with extensive experience and knowledge to do the job but who exhibits the wrong behaviors, I would take the untrained person any time. Skills and knowledge on their own will not make a successful selection—they can be provided with training and development—but innate values, motives, and intents determine whether ability will manifest itself as consistently displayed behavior.

Developing Behavioral Competencies in Your Unique Organization

The next chapter (*Chapter 4: Developing Behavioral Profiles that Benchmark Top Performance*) will discuss critical incidents, focus groups, behavioral profiles, and how to turn them into a successful behavioral interview. But first, I would like to stress the importance of developing behavioral competencies and a concept of fit that is suited to the specific needs and circumstances of your organization.

To illustrate this point, let's consider a negative example. We are all familiar with the phrase, "learning as you go," a competency listed in a popular, generic, profile system. At first glance, this competency seems reasonable. Organizations and markets change quickly; therefore, it makes sense that in order to be successful in our organization an employee must be able to "learn as you go." But if that is truly a success factor in your organization, then, no doubt, your employee who exhibits that behavior will do equally well in a wireless phone company, the CIA, a school district in Pennsylvania, or a chip manufacturing plant in Taiwan: Learning as you go is key in these diverse organizations too. It sounds ridiculous, and it is.

As this example illustrates, off-the-shelf competencies fail because they often don't convey the values of the organization. An organization that develops its competencies using off-the-shelf products is hampered from the get-go and bound to fail in the long run without significant modification and customization to the corporate business plan and actual values.

In order to achieve an organization's strategic goals, our best bet is to hire people who fit the value-behaviors of the organization and to train people who are not as good a fit to become better. Selecting, developing, recognizing, and rewarding behaviors that are explicitly valued by the organization will reinforce and support the organization's vision. Those who are not comfortable with the organization's values will experience personal resistance and will not be able to perform well under the circumstances. Top performers, on the other hand, are more likely to be retained and to excel. The majority will be influenced by the new hires who fit the values and behaviors desired by the organization. The new people will lead by example; and become role models for others to follow.

A Road Map for Success

Establishing and using behavioral competencies has great impact on the clarity and fairness of the way employees are rewarded and recognized in the organization. When competencies are the defining measure of success, assessment of an individual employee's performance is no longer linked to personal bias. Rather, all employees are assessed by the same criteria, independent of their manager's feelings towards them.

Successful performers are distinguished by the way they behave in the workplace to achieve desired business results. Since competencies are measurable, they provide extremely objective and helpful information in performance management systems, multi-source assessments, personal review, or training and development interventions.

Even more important, for individual employees, knowing what behavioral competencies are required by a role provides all the information they need to be successful in an organization. Competencies, by their very descriptions, define what constitutes successful performance in key jobs or job families, thus creating a common currency of language throughout the organization. Those wanting to advance in their careers need only look at their own competency profile and compare it to the profile of a level or position they wish to attain. What better way can an organization motivate and reward its employees than by encouraging them to actively and independently develop the capabilities the organization needs to achieve its vision?

If the competencies are well defined and truly lived by the organization, they provide a road map for employees to be consistently successful. They allow people to act without having to refer to the rule book since competencies are the foundation for the rules. They, in fact, answer the question each employee wants answered, "What exactly do I have to do to be successful?" Write your competencies based on your business plan and on your real, lived values, and you will have the foundation for an integrated human resources process that brings your people into alignment with your strategy.

Working With Values: Case Study Examples

All of the case studies we have profiled used organizational values as an intrinsic element of defining *fit* in order to bring cohesiveness to their behavioral interviewing systems. Some drove their profile development work forward by turning their values into concrete behavioral statements that, in effect, described how those values were manifested. Other more established organizations checked the behavioral competencies of a role against their values as a way of confirming their accuracy and validity.

Calgary Police Service

Dale Burns of the Calgary Police Service put together its original competency assessments by cutting and pasting phrases found in external organizations. Although this served a purpose in increasing general awareness about competencies, Dale didn't feel that it was truly reflective of the organization, because it wasn't developed by the people doing the work, and it wasn't validated.

In developing behavioral competencies in-house, Dale turned to a values exercise to determine competencies based on the organization's values. He then polled everyone in the organization to determine what was important to them. The following chart shows the level of response.

Number of Validation Questionnaires Sent and Returned[7]			
Profile	Number Sent	Number Returned	Response Rate
Constable	942	265	28.1%
Detective	139	70	50.4%
Sergeant	130	57	43.8%
Staff Sergeant	57	39	68.4%
Inspector	62	38	61.3%
Totals:	1330	469	35.3%

Note: questionnaires were sent to all individuals of a particular rank and their supervisors.

Through this work, the Calgary Police Service defined seven core values that were clearly identified for the first time. In focus groups and training sessions, all members of the service helped to further refine and define the values, and then developed corresponding competency profiles for job families within the organization. In this way, the values of the Calgary Police Service were translated into clearly stated behaviors that formed the basis not only of a new approach to promotion and succession planning, but also of revamped hiring, performance management, and career development procedures.

As Dale describes, "It's a big ship and it's hard to turn around over night but it's starting to work, yes, and we've carried this thing pretty far."

"We've now identified the core competencies required to be a member of the Calgary Police Service right in the recruit package. When recruit applicants come in, we do a full behavioral interview with the applicant, seeking both the competencies and the values that you are required to possess. I really think that we are now hiring people that have the competencies required to excel, that they

---

[7] David Cohen, Claire Moncrieff, based on research—unpublished article.

share our values, they go through training based on those values and competencies and when they hit the street their annual performance assessment is based on the behaviors, the competencies, and the values.

"So now our learning center and our recruit training curriculum is based on values. We have values-based training. In the old style, we taught it in class: here's a summons, here's how you write a summons, not why. We now go into here's how and here's why. Here's the value of writing a summons and issuing a caution. People know why it's important now.

"The transfer competition and promotional processes are all based on the same. And there's a real nice mix now. I'm still working on the performance appraisals, in the final stages, but we've tied the behavioral component into the development plan and its directly linked to our business plan. So it's all part of the mission, vision, and values."

Sprint Canada

At Sprint Canada, Victoria Walker, like Dale, also started from the ground up.

"It started out as a visioning exercise. At that time the company was developing its vision and values and from that we stemmed off into success profiles. Before we did our interviewing, we pulled out what we considered to be our best characteristics as indicated by our four values just to understand what we mean when we talk about our values—how do our best employees portray them in the workplace? That took a fair bit of time, and out of that we developed a list of what we called *Values Best Practices*. So for each of our values we had maybe 25 statements that anybody could read and immediately try to emulate, that would help exemplify our values.

"Then after that we developed the behavioral competency profiles for job families in the organization. We used all that work that we did with the values and incorporated it so that with every job family we put each of the four value statements in there in a way that it related specifically to that job. As an example, obviously innovation, for instance, which is one of our values, would relate very differently to a customer service rep than it would to a director; we made sure we had each of those four values woven in, but woven in an appropriate way.

"So we took that process out to focus groups, employee groups, and got a lot of extensive feedback to make sure that what we crystallized them down into, say 25 to 50 statements, each success profile would represent each job family. They were clustered under a series of about 12 of the most behavioral characteristics, always four of which would be our core values."

Abbott Labs

At Abbott Labs, Andrée Charbonneau says that values were used as a way of clarifying and honing the behavioral statements when competencies were identified. Coming from using an off-the-shelf competency toolkit, it was quite interesting to go through the exercise of determining what really distinguished the organization and how that was manifested in the way work was done.

"We completely redefined the profile when we went back to the drawing board and said, 'okay, customer focus in the pharmaceutical representative, what does that really look like in action?' How is Abbott different from a Merck or an Eli Lilly? Would somebody know this by looking at this particular competency profile? This involved a significant amount of discussion," Andrée adds. "It is not immediately clear."

HMV Canada

Marnie Falkiner found that the work done at HMV Canada on behavioral profiles reinforced an already strong culture. "The culture was strong to begin with. It was very clear. It was written down and then it was reflected in the performance review and the profiles as well, so it had a life of its own. It talked about being enterprising, having voice, being creative, having autonomy, delivering high performance, and being responsible."

But she was concerned that when senior people left the organization, the culture was going to go with them. "It didn't. It was self-perpetuating because it was built into everything. We hired, reviewed, rewarded that way, so it came to be really strong in the organization."

Michelin North America

At Michelin North America, Milan Mizerovsky saw the power of concrete behavioral statements and their reflection of core values most clearly during the later development of a performance management system.

"One of the things that evolved out of this process at the same time was that we were looking, as most organizations do every four years, at an evolution of the performance management process. Through discussions and through the success of behavioral interviewing it seemed to make sense to say, well, if these are our criteria for success here, could we do a similar process and identify criteria for success that we could then utilize within the performance management process? In 10 or 12 focus groups, we identified within the organization the kinds of things people were doing who were noted for performing particularly well. We then took a look at how that success was defined and examined those behaviors in order to differentiate the average performers from the top.

"Going into it—this to me was perhaps one of the most interesting things—we anticipated that, in fact, we would have two appraisal forms and two sets of behavioral descriptions, one managerial/professional and another plant employee. In fact, what we saw was that the criteria were so similar that there was nearly an 80 percent overlap. The words that were used were perhaps a little bit different, but the actual behaviors were essentially the same. As a result, we ended up having one system. And that was not what we went in thinking we would do. We had figured there would be two.

"You have to remember this was close to 10 years ago. It would have been relatively unheard of at that point to have one performance appraisal process throughout the organization. And our sense was that the power of that far outweighed a few things that applied to managers and didn't apply to others, so we decided to just add those in rather than have two forms. We felt that this sent a very powerful message that all employees have similar kinds of behaviors leading to success, though they may get manifested a little bit differently."

Starbucks

When she moved from Thomas Cook to Starbucks, Christine Deputy had the opportunity to look at an entirely different organizational culture involved in a very different marketplace and to see first-hand how an organization's values are intrinsic to its success and growth.

"I came to Starbucks, and we're so much bigger, more than 2,800 stores in North America. One of the things we were quite curious about was, is there consistency across all of the different geographic areas or do you see differences in the behaviors that make you successful in Manhattan versus the behaviors that make you successful in Dallas? What we found was, there isn't. There aren't differences. It is incredibly consistent. What we're finding now as we look international is you can talk to partners in Japan and we're finding the same thing. And that's the dynamic of the brand and the values associated with it.

"You do value work when you do these focus groups and talk to employees about organizational values. At Thomas Cook, we were all over the map because we had done all these different acquisitions. Within Starbucks, the personal and corporate values are right there and consistent. During focus groups you asked participants not just to repeat mission and value statements, but what do you think we're really about? And they went to the flipchart and told us, and it was always the same.

"The thing that we've been worried about as we go into this next phase of our growth is that we've been very high touch in our cultural transmission, very very anecdotal. Partners all have their own little stories and they share their experiences and about how we grew up; it's very relationship focused. The concern is that as we grow, the people who are telling the stories are farther away from the heart of the organization. What we're finding, however, is that we are getting a strong level of transmission, because the culture is strong and the values consistent. However, we are still trying to overlay the processes to help make sure that we stay really focused and really solid because, though we get the sense of it and the feel of it, we need to ensure that we get the delivery of it."

Christine finds, that using the profile work helps tremendously. It serves as a delivery mechanism for transmitting values across geography, time, and new generations of employees.

"There's a state of clarity and understanding and consistency of language with this. For a large organization that's growing very quickly or with any organization that has multiple acquisitions, there will always be a danger of a lack of clarity around values. This kind of tool can help create a common language. When you have common language, then you can change behavior. Without that, you can't get at that many people in a multi-location environment. You can't turn the boat because it's too diffused."

Summary

As these case studies reveal, clearly defined and articulated values are essential to successful organizations. When an organization's values are clear, they permeate and define each employee's behavior—from top managers to plant workers. In healthy organizations, these values are expressed daily, through myriad actions and are key to top performance. For those facing the challenge of hiring new people, finding the right fit between your organization, the job, and the candidate's skills and behaviors is the key to hiring right. Behavioral interviewing provides the structure for describing jobs in terms of the values and behaviors of your organization. It also provides the means for interpreting candidates' behaviors, not just their experience. Next, we'll look at the nuts and bolts of putting behavioral interviewing into action.

Developing Behavioral Profiles that Benchmark Top Performance

Identifying, Examining, and Describing Top Performance

A behavioral interview is based on a thorough understanding of the organization in general and the job in particular. In this chapter we will look at the process of doing an accurate, full-circle examination of how work is accomplished by top performers who are acting in accordance with the organization's values and strategic needs.

Human resources—whether a trained corps or a few individuals—leads the facilitation of focus groups in order to gain a thorough and accurate understanding of the nature of top performance. Once those behavioral competencies have been identified, they must be defined and written in language that is concrete, precise and in tune with the organization's terminology and lingo. Once this is done, the behavioral profile is validated by those directly affected by the descriptions. Once the behavioral profile is in place, it is translated into questions within an interview guide, which is to be used by those leading the actual hiring process. In accomplishing these steps, human resources lays out the road map for how the organization can achieve its strategic goals through its people.

Management has a great responsibility in supporting this process from the early stages of defining the behavioral competencies to the final goal of using them properly in recruitment and selection. Developing behavioral profiles through focus groups requires energy, time and commitment which must be supported, every step of the way, by management. Using those behavioral profiles in the interview process involves training and discipline as well as dedication to following the structured procedures. The work, however, is of almost incalculable benefit to the organization as a whole and the stakeholders of the job in question. Engaging in a thorough examination of what defines top performance enlists the minds of all those involved in the work. It requires that the job be considered from all perspectives in order to pinpoint the key performance indicators—the actual job actions that an employee will take in order to successfully demonstrate the best way of working. Hiring and promoting the use of these terms sends a clear message that top performance is recognized and rewarded. There is no better way for the organization to communicate how to be successful than to focus intently on what is needed to achieve strategic goals. Consequently, the profile can also be integrated into the performance management process.

For the majority of employees, clearly written behavioral profiles are a godsend. They are not a set of unrealistic or unreasonable performance dimensions inflicted, like punishment, from the senior executive. Rather, the definition of top performance itself comes through the consensus of those doing the work and is defined in terms that they understand and find meaningful. In this way, a measuring stick has been laid out for all to see that indicates clearly, not only what it takes to be successful in the organization, but how to do so.

Critical Incidents

A behavioral profile is composed of a number of individual and isolated behavioral competency statements that indicate one aspect of how success on the job is achieved. The key to identifying these competencies—and understanding the nature of top performance—is to examine work through the framework of the "critical incident."

In "The Critical Incident Technique," a seminal paper about performance written in 1954, John C. Flanagan outlined the method best used for understanding the nature of top performance. A critical incident, according to Flanagan, is a moment of activity "sufficiently complete in itself to permit inferences and predictions about the person performing the act."[1] As Flanagan relates, in order to define behavioral competencies, we must first identify a critical incident, which exemplifies key aspects of top performance.

Most of us think about a role or job in terms of tasks and outcomes, described in the last chapter as the "what" of a job. We rarely consider what it takes to accomplish a task or achieve an outcome—"the how" of a job—and yet this is the vital piece of information needed to understand what separates failure from success or average performance from superior.

Critical incidents clarify the "how" of a job. Nevertheless, a distinction must be made. Critical incidents are not interested in just any aspect of a job but rather those key times that somehow typify what it really takes to excel and achieve organizational goals. The difference is illuminating. In the average workday we are confronted with numerous duties, most of which are common and unremarkable but important in accomplishing the job. Behavioral competencies, however, must describe performance that is exceptional rather than average or status quo, otherwise it will reinforce mediocre performance instead of pointing the way to achievement and future development. Critical incidents, therefore, focus on those moments when key outcomes are on the line and certain

---

[1] John C. Flanagan, "The Critical Incident Technique," *Psychological Bulletin*, 51 No. 4 (1954): 327-355.

behaviors lead to greater (and more strategically aligned) success than others. They do so by defining the circumstances of those moments, the underlying behaviors used to manage the situation, and the resulting outcome.

A Critical Incident: An Example

As a hypothetical example, consider the following:

In a small software start-up, an inside sales representative phoned a customer in the company database to let her know about a new product offer. The customer replied that her last experience with the company was a negative one and she wasn't interested in any more products. Disappointed, the sales representative asked what had happened and learned that, though the product had a major flaw, the support department had been unresponsive. Consequently, the customer gave up on the product and the company in frustration.

The sales representative knew he had several options. Under the gun for monthly quotas, he could make note of the problem in the database and move on to a more receptive customer. Or, he could go to a lot of effort and get to the bottom of the problem personally and see if he could salvage the client's business.

On his own time, the sales representative approached the director of customer service about the problem. Together, they reviewed the file to further understand the situation and decide how to approach it. The inside sales representative called the customer back a few days later and negotiated with her to allow a software consultant to visit her office, free of charge, to rectify the previous situation. The success of that visit led to future business with the client. Commission for the sales lead went to the inside sales representative.

Breaking Down the Incident

It is important to understand what the actions are that led to success in this situation.

- The circumstance in question was that the sales representative made a standard sales call to a repeat customer who happened to have an unresolved problem with the company's product and service

- The outcome of the circumstance was that the customer was satisfied and new business was generated

It is easy to see that understanding merely the circumstance and outcome doesn't give us tremendous insight into how the outcome came about, nor whether the road leading to it was one worth pointing out and emulating. Sure, the sales representative "handled the customer effectively," but how? To get a better understanding of this, we need to look at the underlying behaviors that resulted in the outcome.

In this particular case, the sales representative listened to the customer's problem, temporarily dealt with her frustration, and brought the problem to the attention of someone in the organization. He took ownership by following through on his own time with customer service. He showed commitment in getting back to the person and facilitated a stop-gap resolution by clearly understanding the client's perspective. Furthermore, on a second call he negotiated with the customer to get to the next stage in dealing with the problem. And it was these combined efforts that led to the organization's obtaining new business.

The Right Critical Incident and Behaviors

Was this example, however, a critical incident? It's impossible to know without understanding the values, vision, and strategic mission of the organization. It takes skill to identify and analyze a critical incident in the context of your organization. Not every work-related circumstance points to behaviors that are really necessary for the organization to achieve its strategic goals. It is important to understand the way organizational values, vision, and business strategy interlink as the contextual background for behavioral interviewing. Why? The culture of the organization is driven behaviorally at its core by values that transcend a particular position. The right candidate is therefore a fit for both the position and the organization as a whole. Only a person with the appropriate attributes will consistently respond in the right ways to the issues which your organization finds strategically critical.

In order to determine which behaviors are worth using as indicators of top performance, we need to ask a number of validation questions regarding any particular critical incident.

- Did the behaviors meet the organization's values?
- Were they in line with business strategy and the overall vision the organization wants to achieve?
- Was the new business that was captured strategically important?

In the case of the sales representative, if the organization wants to raise revenue per customer while not losing customers to the competition, the sales representative might have exhibited skills worthy of a top performer. But if the organization was not interested in that kind of customer anymore or does not tolerate "wasting" time and opportunity in dealing with such a problem, that behavior might not have been right. Furthermore, we have to examine how the behavior manifested itself. Was it accompanied by complaint or criticism? Did it reduce the morale of the customer service department or did it support their efforts? The truth is in the details. Competencies must be in line with the values of the organization and in coherence with both the short-term business plan and the long-term vision.

Critical Incidents and Behavioral Interviewing

In the interview itself, the process is to discover how well each individual candidate matches his or her past behaviors to the desired behaviors listed in the profile. Again, behavioral competencies are not indicators of average or status quo performance. That is why, when sifting through circumstances, outcomes, and underlying behaviors, we search for extreme moments to examine.

All challenges are not created equal: some are more key to making the business strategy happen; others promote innovation, require more of our talents, stretch us further, unleash creativity, or are particularly difficult. Tell us about the best team that you ever participated in; what made it special? What was your most critical challenge in dealing with supply and how did you solve it? What were the circumstances of your most successful sales call, and what did you do to make it so successful? By exploring extreme moments, we begin to understand what separates those who excel in a position from those who merely hold it.

The behavioral profiles developed through critical incidents provide the foundation for understanding what the organization really needs, now and in the future, in order to make its business strategy happen—better, faster, more effectively.

However, the benefits are not limited to hiring new employees. For current employees locked into status quo performance, behavioral profiles provide guidance by leveraging the organization's own stated best practices to catapult average performers to higher levels of performance.

Focus Groups

The importance of identifying critical incidents and their underlying behaviors through focus groups cannot be overstated. Focus groups are used because no one person is well versed enough in all aspects of a job to grasp and articulate everything that it takes to be successful in that position. Focus groups are composed of a variety of key stakeholders, possibly including, for example, current occupants of the role, supervisors and managers, peers or colleagues, and even internal and external customers. Within such a context, critical incidents are examined, top performers are identified, and a rigorous discussion ensues to determine the underlying behaviors that led to success in the situation at hand. The information and consensus becomes the data for developing grounded behavioral profiles.

When using focus groups to generate the data that leads to the profile, one concern is that an influential individual will lead others to think the same way or one powerful person will shut down honest conversation. Another concern when using the focus group approach is that the conversation will become a complaint session about the company, reinforcing, if not spreading, negative feelings. The role of the facilitator is to maintain a rigorous focus on the task at hand. The objective of the discussion is to build success in the company by discovering what concretely needs to be done, ie., the correct behaviours for success. A focused facilitator will help you avoid the negativity of some people and the overbearing influence of others.

How to Make Them Work

When determining who should comprise a focus group, it is necessary to consider what kind of information you are looking for. If you talk to the wrong people, you can end up with competencies that may look impressively behavioral but are based on the wrong information and are therefore not true predictors of current, let alone future, desired success. Customers must be key customers, those whose business you really want to capture. Current occupants of the role should be top performers or those who otherwise have some kind of special insight into what defines top performance. Peers should be those who really depend on the incumbent for the quality of their own work. Managers and supervisors must be those who are moving their groups towards achieving the organization's desired business strategy, as well as those known for their ability to develop successful contributors in that role.

Some Common Pitfalls

It is tempting to save the time and effort of all involved by having the HR professional observe work directly or interview key stakeholders one at a time, and then write a behavioral profile based on that data. Doing so will not capture the essence of top performance—what it really takes to get a job done—because it will not be validated by rigorous discussion about the nature, purpose, and processes of the job.

Another temptation is to translate or adapt behavioral profiles from one situation to another, without using focus groups for each new job profile. The thinking is that once the work of developing a behavioral profile for a position in one part of the company has been done, it is expedient to adapt that to roles in other parts of the company. The pressure to do so can be immense. Supervisors, executives, and area managers will see an opportunity to replicate in cookie-cutter fashion what worked well through in-depth analysis. Resist this pressure. It's true that there should be significant areas of overlap across a company with a common culture, but the indicators of top performance will be particular to each role. Without a full-circle examination of the particular critical incidents related to each role or job family, success rates will be significantly lower. Cases in which organizations acted intuitively to save time in developing profiles for other areas of the organization have led to a weakening of results and higher rates of turnover than in areas where the work was done properly and thoroughly.

Benchmarking the competencies of your competitors and using those as your model is useless as well. What's the common sense behind that statement? There are no other organizations with the same values, business plan, or market that you have. If there were, that organization would probably buy your company or your company would buy them! For example, what makes a good entry-level engineer in your organization won't necessarily match what it takes to succeed somewhere else. Benchmarking studies that supposedly span dozens or hundreds of organizations make competencies generic to the point where they become meaningless. Who cares what others in your industry have done? It does not validate your approach to how you do business. Benchmarking is only effective to validate the process of what you do when that process is repetitive and can be reproduced by you.

Likewise, off-the-shelf competencies are also a dead end. Alhough such tools may be appealing to HR, employees won't buy into them because they don't match the language used on the job, nor can they even hope to pinpoint the nuances of successful performance unique to your organization. Rather than expand the discussion to encompass what it truly takes to succeed in the organization, a focus group centering around pre-packaged competencies will confine employees to developing profiles based only on the context of the behaviors presented to them. The most important areas of concern might be entirely overlooked. Ask yourself: Is the output of a generic list of competencies going to capture the uniqueness of your corporate culture and the ways you do business?

Facilitators

Facilitators of focus groups must be well-trained in order to skillfully guide a wide-open debate on what constitutes top performance. They need the sensitivity to be able to manage disparate elements and ask the right questions that engage them in revealing how they've done their work. As well, facilitators must possess the hard-nosed organizational knowledge to recognize and handle the often tough information that emerges about who is doing his or her job right and under what circumstances.

In the actual focus group, the facilitator asks the members to think of the best people they have known in the job in question. What were those top performers doing in comparison to less successful incumbents? What was it that they achieved? How did they go about doing the job differently to make that success happen? Each circumstance is examined for its outcome and underlying behaviors. A list of instances linked to concrete actions begins to be collected.

This is the time in which doing detailed in-house work really pays off compared to using generic lists of competencies. As an example, a major retailer was having difficulties with the generic competency used to define the nature of creativity in its art department. In fact, the competencies currently being used were inherently contradictory because behaviors acceptable under one heading were not allowed under another. This sent mixed messages, provoked frustration with the profile, and threatened to make the behavioral interviewing process feel illegitimate to the people who needed to use it.

Through information unearthed in more detailed focus group work it was discovered that there were actually two aspects of creativity indicative of the kinds of top performers the organization needed. On the one hand, there were those people who have unique ideas, but cannot apply them to a business context. On the other hand, there were those who can take other people's unique ideas and successfully apply them to business. Accordingly, the single, generic competency for creativity was divided into two distinct and necessary behaviors: creative innovation and creative application. Arriving at these behaviours through a focus group engaged people in the process and captured what truly made the company unique and successful.

A good facilitator understands the values and vision of the organization and is able to grasp how business strategy is actualized in day-to-day operations. He or she is skilled in identifying situations that lead to achieving business strategy and isolating what was key about those moments in order to go after the behaviors involved. The facilitator must be able to conduct debate, achieve consensus and validate the behaviors that are finally decided on by identifying other examples where they came into play. It's a demanding role, but there is nothing more essential for developing meaningful behavioral profiles—the keystone for a successful behavioral interviewing system.

Conducting a Focus Group

- Select participants who have demonstrated the right behaviors as a means for achieving the desired results—the ones that you wish you could clone
- Send participants an invitation explaining that they are invited to participate in a discussion regarding what defines success in their role

- In preparation for the meeting, ask participants to consider:
  1. What actions they have taken when learning new ways of doing things on the job and new information
  2. How they detect and solve problems
  3. If they make decisions, how they make them
  4. How they communicate, both inside and outside the organization, both in large groups and one-on-one
  5. What motivates them personally
  6. How they are motivated by others
  7. How they solve conflict
  8. How they organize their work
- Set aside three hours for the discussion
- Begin the focus group by explaining why you are doing it
- Ensure you clearly articulate the application for the profile
- Consistently focus on asking participants what actions they took to achieve the desired results
- Arrange for someone to take notes

Identifying Must-Have and Preferred Behavioral Competencies

As behavioral data is gathered, patterns emerge and the list of actions can be whittled down into categories with a number of examples.

The hard work of focus groups will unearth a lot of great information about what it takes to be successful in the organization. It is tempting to use all of this knowledge when writing the behavioral profile and the subsequent interview questions. As in most things, however, keeping it simple is best. Having too many behavioral competencies associated with a role invites deselection more than selection. By making the fit for a role too precise, you will be eliminating many who could be top performers but who simply do not have the complete set of behaviors you have identified. If, for example, a focus group ultimately determines that top performers are characterized by 12 separate behaviors, those behaviors must be narrowed down. I suggest that three to six competencies are all that are needed to describe any position, no matter its complexity or rank. Each of those behaviors should in turn have only four to five attributes or expressions. Call them knock-out points. If a candidate has these attributes he or she can excel at the job and learn the rest over time. Please refer to the sample profile on page 91.

Helpful Tips for Focus Group Questioning

- Introductory Statement: *We are specifically studying how people are successful in your specific role. We believe you're especially well-qualified to tell us this.*

- Request for Specific Information: *What would you say is the primary drivers of success when achieving results?*

- Request for Summary: *Can you summarize our discussion in a few words?*

It is important to distinguish those competencies that are essential to the job from those that are merely nice to have. Must-have competencies are those that a candidate must have prior to being hired. Preferred competencies are those that can be developed once on the job. Preferred competencies tend to be more easily influenced by technical training or personal development plans. Must-have competencies reflect organizational values and business objectives, both of which are unique to your company.

If a person doesn't possess your must-have competencies he or she will not fit into the organization no matter how skilled, experienced, or accomplished. Remember, though, that not everyone will exhibit all of the competencies in a particular role. Go for the core—the behaviors that reflect organizational values and the basic knock-out points required to start the job—and train the rest.

Narrowing your focus is a critical exercise in determining what it really takes to be successful in the organization. Many managers have difficulty doing this. They want candidates who can do everything. But it serves no purpose to expect too much; it only reduces the talent pool unnecessarily.

Writing the Behavioral Profile

From the focus groups, the facilitator determines what constitutes the key indicators of successful job actions. Translating this understanding into clear terms and descriptions is both a skill and an art. The ability to do so improves with deliberate practice and time. It is necessary to always be concrete and to ensure that behavioral statements include the outcome and the behavior involved in precise terms.

How to Write Effective Profiles

A skillfully written behavioral profile incorporates terminology, reference points, and even slang used by those holding the position. After all, it is not HR or the OD team who has to own, adapt to, and live the behaviors in question but the technicians and engineers in the petroleum products division or the client managers in the retail branches. Using the concrete language of the line ensures that the profile will be meaningful to all—from supervisors and current stakeholders to future candidates—and gives everyone a stronger grasp of what it takes to succeed.

It's important to be consistent across an organization. If a corporation has defined its values, then the behaviors needed for success are the same within job families and across geographic or business unit boundaries. The language describing behaviors may vary, but the terms of success should overlap. For this reason, you should not take the chance of letting managers in different regions come up with behaviors that are not the same. If you leave the profile development solely up to each area manager in San Francisco, Chicago, and Boston, they may be diligent and thorough but will no doubt fail to articulate identical behaviors, either because they lack the big picture or do not have as many examples to draw on.

People will be hired for the same position in different regions for different reasons. Picture the national sales convention. At dinner, a regional sales person complains about his or her review, "I was marked negatively on teamwork this year." Another says, "That's funny, I did better on teamwork this year than last." They start to compare notes and find out that their managers are defining teamwork differently. The organization as a whole may have a new push on teamwork as a competency in need of development, but the way it's described is inconsistent.

It is also important to keep behavioral profiles current. They should be reviewed every four to five years to make sure that they are still apt, accurate, and necessary. During periods of rapid organizational change, however, key behaviors may quickly diminish in importance or previously unimportant behaviors may suddenly become vital. Mapping out how change is expected to affect the strategy of an organization can help you keep your eyes open for that kind of evolution.

Validating helps. Once you've written a draft, redistribute the behavioral profiles to the members of the focus group or even to the organization as a whole. People will respond viscerally as to whether the profile is clear and adequately describes their role or whether it is vague, confusing, irrelevant, or not specific to the right behaviors. You may have to dig in and edit what you have produced from your notes to develop a profile that more accurately reflects reality, but it's worth it because including others in the process builds consensus and acceptance.

Some Common Pitfalls

When actually writing profiles, there are some common weaknesses to look out for. Most profiles I read are based on outcome statements, not behaviors. Recall the critical incident example about the inside sales representative for the software company. To say that a key competency in that organization is to "handle customers effectively" does not even come close to describing the behaviors that were detailed in the critical incident. Only by defining those behaviors that led to that result can we hope to understand how success is manifested and then predict whether a candidate can perform similarly once on the job.

The value of such a strict concrete approach transfers directly into the interview as well. In an interview, if you ask someone if he or she is a leader or has integrity, you will get a certain kind of answer. If, on the other hand, you ask him or her to tell you about a time when he or she showed leadership or integrity, a specific story would emerge that can be probed in greater detail to determine if there is a good fit with the organization's explicit definition of integrity or leadership.

In writing profiles, there is a tendency to be vague and generic in our language even when we are dealing with concrete behaviors. For example, the words "demonstrates" or "ability to" often appears in a behavioral description, but they are sure signs that the profile is poorly written. To say that someone "demonstrates active listening by allowing others to express their ideas..." explains very little. Whether a behavior is demonstrated or not is a decision that you have to make based on an analysis of the circumstances and outcome. Try this exercise in remedy. Take the word "demonstrates" and the three words that follow it out of the description and then start with the adjective or verb. For example, "demonstrates the ability to actively listen" can be changed to "actively listens to others, allowing them to finish their thought prior to responding." Chances are that what is left behind is a more concrete version of the behavior you are trying to describe.

Poorly written behavioral statements lead to confusion. Good behavioral statements include the "how" of a behavior with the outcome. Saying that someone "takes initiative," "follows through," or "treats customers with respect" tells us almost nothing about what that person actually did. In a behavioral statement, we need to define how a person takes initiative, follows through, or treats a customer with respect, and what doing so accomplishes.

There is also a danger that skillful writers may find it too easy to use language that sounds "behavioral" without necessarily describing the right behaviors in the right ways. Skill with language is no substitute for hard analysis. As Andrée Charbonneau of Abbott Labs has remarked, "You can be a whiz at taking a traditional question and reformatting it as a behavioral question, but if it's not linked to the competencies that matter in your organization, it's not going to work." It helps to stick to the model for behavioral statements in a disciplined way—i.e., all behavioral statements must be backed up with real examples of how that key behavior is exhibited.

Sample Behavioral Profile

The following is a sample profile of an entry-level engineer. All sample profiles should be approached with caution because they are generic descriptions which are not tied to any organization. While it is important to understand how a profile looks, it is useless to emulate one without going through the process of developing it in focus groups in accordance with your organization's own unique values and strategy.

Six behavioral competencies were identified in the profile of an entry-level engineer. The ideal engineer was determined to be:

1. Decisive problem solver
2. Client focused
3. Communicator
4. Results oriented
5. Networker and relationship builder
6. Innovative and creative

These competencies on their own do not describe enough to be useful. When writing them into a behavioral profile, we expand on what we have learned in the focus groups, making that information more specific and concrete and using key words to clearly describe what a top performer would do behaviorally in different circumstances. The following sample shows how competencies translate into behaviors:

Decisive Problem Solver

- Gathers, organizes, and evaluates information, balancing the pros and cons according to the desired outcome
- Develops recommendations for action that best serve the overall objectives of the organization and the project

An entry-level engineer who is a decisive problem solver:

- Quickly obtains needed technical information from the most logical internal or external source when assigned an unfamiliar or challenging task
- Retains information and experience gained from the application of new information when solving a problem
- Detects deviations from standards by reviewing maintenance reports and probing for additional detail
- Projects the future impact of a current minor deviation and takes corrective action prior to problems becoming major difficulties
- Continuously reviews equipment and procedures, suggesting efficient changes to design and layout that cut down on working distance, reduce mechanical failures, and result in improved workflow, lower production costs, better quality, and higher levels of safety

Client Focused

- Develops and maintains strong relationships with internal customers
- Uses understanding of customer needs, desires, and critical success factors to influence priorities, initiatives, and objectives
- Anticipates customer needs and responds with appropriate and helpful solutions

An entry-level engineer who is client focused:

- Directly involves line staff in problem identification and exploration of alternative ideas

- Uses a language understood by the line staff avoiding any and all academic or highly technical words or jargon
- Gives credit at all levels of the company for line suggestions used in solving problems
- Willingly rolls up shirt sleeves to experience the nitty-gritty details of production problems from the line perspective, taking the time to work on the line during all production shifts
- Asks questions to discover new information with an open mind, reserving conclusions for when all information has been collected

Communicator

- Takes advantage of opportunities to listen to others and to satisfy their need for information
- Provides information and exchanges ideas in a way that promotes open communication and understanding
- Shares information clearly and concisely—in accordance with the level of understanding of the audience and without holding back information necessary to others

An entry-level engineer who is a communicator:

- Communicates clearly and directly either one-on-one or to a specific audience, using widely accepted company terminology and simple analogies that make the point in terms understood by the audience
- Checks for audience understanding by asking for feedback and questions that seek additional information
- Asks the other party to summarize to ensure mutual understanding of either the problem, solution, or commitment
- Writes clear, concise, and complete administrative reports and documentation in a language understood by both engineering and the line
- Completes material orders neatly and in detail
- Submits design drawings which are clear, clean, and detailed

- Processes client requests by asking constructive questions that seek to get at the reason for the request and to uncover additional unstated details by asking questions which relate to implications for the request down the line

- Asks questions from perspectives not previously considered by the client to ensure all implications are considered by all concerned, prior to building an action plan

- Persuasively presents process enhancements to the line through logical, enthusiastic, and credible trial performance

- Formulates the presentation in terms of value-added to the floor

- Promptly informs project team and supervisors of all anomalies

Results Oriented

- Demonstrates initiative and strives to continuously achieve higher levels of individual and organizational performance by setting and pursuing goals that are not easily attainable

- Finds ways to improve company's performance

An entry-level engineer who is results oriented:

- Works steadily on assigned projects, finding useful monitoring and recording tasks for each project, even if the project is routine

- Accepts challenging goals and objectives that ensure their professional development

- Provides extra effort by staying late, taking work home, working on weekends, or showing up at all shifts to gain first-hand knowledge and experience of the operations

- Puts overall company objectives ahead of personal objectives, shifting priorities accordingly

- Divides projects into definable tasks, setting time and resource objectives for each task

- Integrates project assignments into own personal goals for development

- Manages time effectively by using planning tools such as calendars, to-do lists, and journals

Networker and Relationship Builder

- Works to build or maintain effective relationships or networks of contacts with internal and external associates whose cooperation is important to present or future success
- Uses a variety of methods to influence, persuade, and productively gain others' commitment to ideas, objectives and changes

An entry-level engineer who is a networker/relationship builder:

- Develops a network of contacts in key departments to facilitate finding the right manager to contact when specific problems arise
- Develops contacts with sister plants to enable the shared development of problems as well as learn from other successes and mistakes
- Develops relationships independently within the company
- Shares the success of the implementation with all those involved
- Finds time to interact with coworkers, formally and informally

Innovative and Creative

- Develops new ways of thinking about situations, problems, or opportunities
- Makes recommendations based on intuition and logic
- Makes connections between "unrelated" information or ideas

An entry-level engineer who exhibits innovative creativity:

- Adapts constructively to changes in technology or markets, evaluating how it affects projects and reestablishing priorities
- Checks out changing environments with a mentor to achieve a proper understanding and get answers quickly

- Offers constructive advice to coworkers having difficulty on the task

- Accepts mistakes as a part of the learning process and finds ways of applying new information to follow-up work or previously unconnected circumstances

- Remains constantly on the lookout for new ideas that result in process improvements and shares those ideas with others

- Assists others in developing ideas about new processes or solutions in their work by engaging them in what-if thinking or playing devil's advocate

- Develops solutions that solve multiple problems and pursues their introduction to the company in a timely fashion

- Displays a willingness to consider alternative solutions

Focus groups will provide you with a rich source of concrete examples to draw on. As you hone the description of your must-have competencies into its essential behavioral elements, you will naturally have many things you want to say about how each competency is manifested. As you've seen in the behavioral profile above, these manifestations become the bullet points describing the behavior.

Case Study Profiles

In all of the organizations that we profiled, focus groups proved key to understanding the nature of the work in question. The information gained from them became the basis for hiring, assessing, and promoting by using behavioral competencies.

Michelin North America

At Michelin Canada, four major constituencies were chosen to make up the focus groups used to examine the nature of top performance in the important entry-level engineering position. Those involved included managers or supervisors of the entry-level engineers, former holders of the position who had recently been promoted, recent hires who had just taken on the position, and current holders of the position who were viewed as promotable.

With the help of a facilitator, consensus was reached as to what people coming into the position were finding most challenging and in need of development. A picture emerged of what distinguished average from exceptional holders of the position, and that picture was compared to the criteria currently being used for selection.

A number of interesting facts were uncovered. Managers, perhaps more distant from the actual work of the entry-level position, were not as clear as others as to what behaviors were necessary for success. One of those key behaviors involved the level of interaction that plant engineers had with plant employees outside of work. Interestingly, those engineers who socialized (on sports teams and at barbecues, for instance) were more apt to be successful in their role. Another characteristic of top performers was their ability to communicate with plant employees. Those who were skilled at direct and forthright communication had better results on their engineering projects than those who weren't. In contrast, those engineers who had recently graduated and used "engineering" terminology were less likely to be successful in projects with line staff. Furthermore, verbal communication skills were a greater indication of success than written skills.

Michelin, a company with a strong engineering tradition, held the belief that a project would be successful because of the intrinsic beauty of the engineering. The technical skills in design were possibly overplayed in comparison to the leadership, communication, and interpersonal skills involved in implementation. In reality, plant engineers who were friendly, social, and clear in their communication were provided with substantially greater levels of support and cooperation from those around them. Employees of such engineers were more open with information, more apt to support decisions, and more willing to work hard. In the end, these, as opposed to technical skills, were the more critical conditions of success.

Understanding these key differentiating factors influenced selection decisions and development tactics. Hiring managers were able to hone in on a candidate's interpersonal and communication style, and supervising managers were able to coach current plant engineers in how to develop needed skills. Defining top performance in concrete behavioral terms allowed managers to be very confident about their analysis during interviews and reviews.

As in most organizations, managers and engineers at Michelin had always known that how work was done was important; but behavioral competencies had never before been articulated openly in a common language. Defining behaviors through focus groups forces the organization to use the language of those on the line to describe how work is done. This was key in opening up consistent dialogue about success, thus developing, in effect, an organizational lexicon of communication. Involving new hires and current holders of the plant engineering position in Michelin's focus groups allowed those people to develop and articulate success in their own terms, in ways that were aligned with the goals of the organization.

Sprint Canada

At Sprint Canada "success" profiles were also designed as the first step towards behavioral interviewing. In order to grasp in its entirety how top performers demonstrated the organization's values in an exemplary fashion, Sprint Canada identified and interviewed best-practice candidates along with their reports and those they reported to. Once behavioral competencies were identified, Sprint Canada took that information to employee focus groups in order to crystallize the data into core statements that were indicative of Sprint Canada's values and meaningful to those doing the work.

As Victoria Walker describes it, "It was surprising how well it went. It really hit home. People wanted to do focus groups. They were very involved in it and really owned the process because the language described so well how they really worked that they could tell it was going to happen. A lot of times you put these initiatives out there and you really have to coax people, and we didn't. Everybody was very into it right from top to bottom."

In writing the profiles Victoria was careful to stick to the organization's culture and focus. The language was "very incorporative of the marketing orientation of the company. We interviewed extensively with the very senior people, including the chairman, the president—all the top people. They had a huge amount of input into the tone and feel of it and they signed off on the whole thing. They're very hands-on in that way and needed to make sure the profiles reflected the language they wanted."

Profiles for the organization covered all positions from vice president down. Victoria believes they were able to get to the core of each job despite the pressures of a rapidly changing environment. "It takes a while to go through that process for one job, and in a very evolving and expanding organization that was a challenge—to keep up with the growth and develop new success profiles. Whole new businesses were coming on board which didn't exist before."

Thomas Cook

At Thomas Cook Christine Deputy led focus groups that were multi-source assessments of the frontline travel consultant position. In this case she included managers, travel consultants, customers, and senior executives who were there to provide a view of the future focus of the organization.

"We asked them to think of their best experiences. Tell me the stories. The focus groups are actually a process by which you collect critical incidents that are, in fact, a series of stories around what happened to make a particular experience so wonderful. You see common stories popping up and you look at what it is the person did and you assign a behavioral description to it."

Christine feels that this story approach is much more effective than direct interviewing. "If you ask what great store managers or great travel consultants do, people can't articulate it, and they give you what they think they should be giving you. When you use critical incident focus groups, it zeroes in on the activities that really made the difference."

Starbucks

At Starbucks, job profiling was done through focus groups on the store manager position. The feedback for this focus group approach has been strongly positive. "They're just fascinated by the level of detail that we can create for this store manager job, how much better and easier it is to work with than what they had before."

Another significant benefit to focus group work arises in the groundswell of support for the methodology, because so many people are involved and have a say in its development. As Christine says, "You can't get credibility in a tool unless people have participated in the development of that tool. There's a high level of communication in a project like this. We did focus groups in all areas with store level partners, store managers, and district managers who they report to, and they were the first ones to receive the actual profile once it was finalized. The feedback was, 'we're so big that we don't always hear what you guys are doing,' but now there's a level of credibility because you've got 100 or 200 people out there who were part of the creation of it and they pre-sell it organizationally. You can't go off and do a little pow wow with 10 people from 10 different areas and think you're going to get the same results."

Writing behavioral profiles, according to Christine, is about "60 percent science, 40 percent art." It helps, she says, to be "doing it with someone else. Part of it is my own personality and style. I couldn't write it alone. I need someone to have a conversation with. You need to go back and forth, make the statement and play with it, because it has to be clear enough that anyone can understand.

"You're trying to tell the story. Think of how some people are really good story tellers. They can make you see what they are describing, the high ceilings of a room, the sun through the windows. You have to do that with behavioral profiles. You have to say, 'What do I see someone doing when I say that?' It needs to be very concrete, very clear with no confusion, nuance, or ambiguity in it. And you have to stay true to the language they gave you in the focus groups. Because if you write it in 'HR speak' or 'corporate speak,' then it doesn't communicate to the people you have to talk to."

Conversely, being good at writing concrete descriptive profiles is not a free pass for skipping focus group work. "I actually did take a stab at it and I wrote a number of statements before I did any of the focus groups and I went back to my boss and said, 'I can't give this to you, it's not right. I don't know if I have the right set of behaviors. There's 150 things these people might be doing. We need to focus on 10. These might be the wrong 10.'"

Calgary Police Service

Dales Burns at the Calgary Police Service had a similar problem with cutting and pasting behavioral descriptions from other organizations—they just didn't fully meet the business plan objectives of the organization, its culture, or the language of those doing the work. To develop behavioral profiles for performance assessment and promotion, he held eight focus groups with top performing constables and also received separate input from sergeants, detectives, staff sergeants, and inspectors. "So we had everybody at every level give some input as to what they thought the behaviors should be for a top-notch constable. We probably interviewed 120 people to develop the job profile."

In his focus groups, however, he was very careful to isolate constituencies from each other so that the dialogue would be more open. "The information we wanted was confidential. We wanted good honest feedback and held these discussions at all levels."

When these profiles were adapted in assessments for promotional purposes and with recruitment drives, the Calgary Police Service began to see a much clearer alignment with its business plan, mission, and overall values.

HMV Canada

At HMV Canada the behavioral approach was originally used for the store manager position to determine what distinguished a successful new manager from those who were a drain on profitability in their first three to four months at a new location. "The average manager," Marnie Falkiner determined, "was trying to prove something to the staff." In effect, they were saying, "'I'm really good, let me show you how to do things right. I'm going to change everything to the way I used to do it in my store and then you'll see the results.' But the staff took it that 'You think my manager before me was lousy and everything we did was wrong'—we would get behavior problems in the store with the staff.

"Average managers didn't know how to accept and listen and learn what the staff in that store was doing. A really successful manager went in and they explored and interviewed and didn't change anything right away and they would slowly see how they could improve the behaviors at the store."

This changed HMV's approach to training, assessing, and selecting for the store manager's position. The work had such an impact on success measures that the use of focus groups was quickly extended to the retail sales positions across the country. "People were so excited to talk to us. They said, 'it's about time you guys ask us what we do.'"

From those focus groups HMV developed its recruitment program. "When you recruit in retail and in the type of business we were in, you were recruiting music lovers. The problem is we would get so hung up on [the need for extensive music knowledge] that we would forget that some of these people had no interpersonal skills and were quite antisocial. We really changed our profile into one where you had to like music and appreciate it, but you didn't necessarily have to be a music-aholic with your own catalogue in your head. So we started hiring people who had interpersonal skills to lead and motivate people and we would, in turn, train them on their music knowledge.

"It really changed the organization from this herd of anti-social music lovers who actually thought there was something wrong with everyone else because they didn't know and appreciate music. I mean these people would build their own personal libraries in the stores and affect inventory levels and would be critical of shoppers. But we changed the profile of who we recruited and developed performance reviews to reflect the profiles."

Using focus groups among so many staff was "hard because the size of the groups was huge. But the information and the credibility were huge too." Still, Marnie found it challenging enough to modify the approach. "When I do them now, we don't necessarily include everyone, but the outcomes are very strong just the same. There were so many people involved that they were asking for the tools before we had time to make them. It wasn't the normal situation when it comes to a new performance review. Usually, it's 'oh yeah, here's something else from HR.'"

The credibility in the assessment, self-training guides, and recruitment profile tools was there from the start "because of the way we did it" involving a wide cross-section of staff in the focus group process.

Another important point Marnie makes, however, is related to what Christine Deputy has also commented on regarding the credibility gained through the use of focus groups. Marnie stresses that communicating the results of the data gained from focus groups is key to getting support for the intervention to follow.

"When you do the focus groups, you learn so much about the organization, but you're the only one who knows it and you have to find a way to get that out." Sometimes, Marnie says, you need to get that information out in a way that is safe for management so that they don't feel chastised by the view points that were given in the open and honest forum of the focus group. You also need to present the information in terms, or perhaps even in forms, that your audience finds meaningful. As Marnie relates, some organization's executives are comfortable with business numbers and anecdotal information, others may require more formal reporting. "You have to understand the world that you're dealing with and know how to talk and present to that world." A mistake in how you sell your own valuable data and plan can set you back with company officers or rank-and-file employees; you have to tailor your message and approach accordingly.

Abbott Labs

At Abbott Labs Andrée Charbonneau examined the competency profiles previously developed with an off-the-shelf system and reinvigorated those descriptions through focus groups.

About using the original off-the-shelf tool she says, "There were competency profiles done for all the key commercial positions and great discipline on the part of managers in terms of using them for selection and behavioral interviewing. It was integrated, too, around the performance management and succession planning exercises. But we got back to the focus group approach anyhow because in discussions on succession planning and the extent to which different candidates met the different competencies, I started realizing the managers were more worried about whether or not this fit the definitions rather than is this what I really need.

"Sometimes [an off-the-shelf] tool can be your worst enemy. They are useful with a skilled user, but there is a great danger of oversimplifying the exercise." Focus groups, on the other hand, do not let you off the hook even when it is difficult to nail down the business issues. "Consensus is the most important thing. Focus groups really add value by forcing the discussion and making sure it happens."

Andrée led the organization through a second exercise and "said basically 'okay, we're going to take the profile as you have laid it out, and we're going to say first of all, is this still true today? And secondly, what does that look like for me?' So if you say 'strategic agility' is a competency for your director of marketing, how would you see strategic agility here in the pharmaceutical products division in that particular position?" This helped managers first understand and then own the profile.

Andrée comments on her experiences in other organizations as well. Regarding the role of the facilitator she is a firm believer that the person running the focus groups must be senior and able to deal with serious business issues that will arise in discussion. "At one organization I was with, we found in certain areas that we had very serious business disagreements. It was really a catalyst for surfacing some important issues. I went back to a couple vice presidents and said, 'look, I can work a sort of middle-of-the-road type profile here that will take everyone's opinion into consideration, but that does nothing about the fact that you've got some general managers who think that this position should be mainly a sales position and others who think that it should be mainly a service position.' Taking a middle-of-the-road approach is going to keep everyone happy but it's not going to solve the problem."

In fact, the company in question was in transition from a government-owned service organization to a privatized and more aggressive sales-oriented one, and that discrepancy reflected the fact that some managers were on the cutting edge, while others retained a more traditional customer orientation. When organizations are in flux, as so many are today, focus groups and behavioral profiles are a way of capturing and creating understanding about the nature of that change and what that means for the organization and the people doing the work. "In that context," Andrée says, "you must say 'look, we've got to change, we've got to do business differently. Well, what does that mean? How do we do that in a way so people will know that they have to do their jobs differently?'"

Changing or communicating clearly and consistently how people are hired, recognized, promoted, and managed will do much to accomplish a shift towards a new direction.

Summary

Behavioral profiles are a powerful tool. By combining an emphasis on overall values and cultural fit with a concrete understanding of what constitutes top performance in a particular job, they enable an organization to capture its most important information: how work needs to be done in order to be successful.

Gathering this information is a rigorous exercise. Focus groups, led by skilled facilitators and involving key stakeholders in the job, are the only way to unearth the information critical to top performance in compliance with organizational values. The process of conducting focus groups encourages wide-spread understanding, acceptance, and use. Since so many in the organization have a stake in the fashioning of the behavioral profiles, their accuracy and relevance to the organization's particular culture is increased dramatically. Even the language used in describing the behavioral profiles will reflect the language of the people doing the work. Defining top performance in this way allows all to use the definition as a measuring stick. Its power cannot be overstated.

CHAPTER 5

Writing Behavioral Questions that Elicit High-Yield Information

Behavioral Questions

The behavioral profile is the foundation for the questions that are asked of the candidate in the interview. Just as a great deal of care must go into translating behavioral information into an accurate profile, so must human resources be very diligent in working with the hiring managers in writing questions that will unearth information pertinent to the profile. The questions should be worded so that the hiring managers can ask them with confidence.

Behavioral questions examine a candidate's actual behaviors in the same way that a focus group looks at top performance. In other words, every behavioral question aims to learn about critical incidents in the candidate's past that are indicative of the behaviors necessary for success on this job. In order to get at such information, we ask about the circumstance (Describe a time when...), the eventual outcome (What was the result...?) and the underlying behaviors

(How did you do...?) in order to determine whether the behaviors the candidate exhibited were the right ones for our needs.

Behavioral questions are written to produce high-yield information. We are interested in critical moments, not status quo or everyday experiences. Accordingly, questions are framed so that they focus on situations that involved the "best, "most," or "biggest" occurrences in a candidate's past. We don't want to find out about a common occasion when a financial services manager solved a client's problems; we want to find out about the time he or she solved the most difficult problem. Asking high-yield questions produces more nuance information and allows for better selection decisions.

Compare the kind of information yielded by a traditional interview using traditional questions to a behavioral interview using behavioral questions. In this case, the concern is to determine whether the candidate is able to work effectively in a team setting.

Traditional Interview

Interviewer:	*Tell me a little about your current activities as they relate to the job you are applying for.*
Candidate:	*I am presently in a client support group. When users call, my job is to find out what the problem is and decide what needs to be done.*
Interviewer:	*So, do you like working with people?*
Candidate:	*Yes, I do. It's a different challenge every day.*
Interviewer:	*What is your understanding about the nature of the position you are applying for in this organization?*
Candidate:	*As I understand it, you are looking for someone to work in your support cell to provide assistance to your users.*
Interviewer:	*And what do you consider to be important qualities for this kind of work?*
Candidate:	*Based on my experience, I'd have to say patience, tact and the ability to communicate clearly. Communication is really key. It's the only way to ensure client satisfaction.*

Interviewer:	*What do you feel are your greatest strengths?*
Candidate:	*I work well in a team and I am very flexible.*
Interviewer:	*What are your weak points?*
Candidate:	*That's always a difficult question. I find it hard to let go of a task and move on when I need to. I must admit that I'm a bit of a perfectionist.*

Behavioral Interview

Interviewer:	*Describe the most effective team that you were part of or led.*
Candidate:	*I was asked to be part of a team that was responsible for conducting an organizational assessment. There were really two teams involved in the initiative, an internal one made up of employees from different departments, and an external one of independent consultants.*
	The purpose of the internal team was to gather all the data and provide an initial assessment. The external team was there to review the data and documentation and then make recommendations to senior management.
Interviewer:	*What was your role exactly?*
Candidate:	*I was the link between the internal and external teams. And I was responsible for organizing an initial training session for the internal team members. They needed to understand the criteria and methodology used for conducting an organizational assessment. After the training, I took the lead in ensuring each member understood what they needed to do in the data collection.*
Interviewer:	*Were there any extraneous circumstances?*
Candidate:	*We had very tight deadlines for this project. When the team met, I went through each task to make sure that every team member could deliver on time, and if not, determine what help they would need. One of the big concerns was that some of the team members' managers still expected them to carry out their full regular workload. I approached my directors about this. We had to do a second*

	presentation to the managers to get their renewed commitment and understanding of the pressures we were under. But even after that, I still had to go after some of the managers again each time we needed access to documentation and data.
Interviewer:	*Did you have any other concerns?*
Candidate:	*The other issue was that there were frequent questions from the internal team for the consultant team. As the link, I took their questions as they arose and always got them responses within the same day. It helped to arrange a regular time for questions and fire off questions and answers by e-mail.*
Interviewer:	*When did this occur?*
Candidate:	*A year ago.*
Interviewer:	*What did you find most challenging?*
Candidate:	*Getting the commitment from managers in general. They gave lip service to the directors but were reluctant when it came down to it to release staff and provide support. It's understandable. We're all under the gun. But that's why we needed the assessment.*
Interviewer:	*How did you overcome these challenges?*
Candidate:	*I put in a lot of time with all the managers promoting the initiative, keeping it in their minds, always reminding them how it would help organizational effectiveness, and benefit them directly.*
Interviewer:	*Why did you consider it the most effective team you were part of?*
Candidate:	*We really came together quickly and in tough circumstances. There were nine of us. We'd never worked together before. But we felt we were doing something important. We managed, despite all the difficulties, to deliver quality results on time. No one on the team fell down. Everyone delivered on their commitments. Whenever someone ran into obstacles, they felt okay about being open with the other team members about it. We managed to resolve things somehow together every time.*

Comparing these two approaches to questioning, it is easy to see how the quality of information differs. We cannot be certain about how to judge the first candidate, since he or she was not really asked questions that elicited quality information. The second candidate, however, has been able to reveal a lot about him- or herself; those answers can be checked against the behavioral profile of the job to see if there is a good fit.

Key Words

We will discuss in detail how to actually conduct a behavioral interview in the next chapter (*Chapter 6: Interviewing to Select and Sell the Best*). In the meantime, however, I want to make a point about how an interviewer uses key words to keep a behavioral profile in mind while listening to a candidate's behavioral answers.

Key words serve as flags to let the interviewer know that the candidate is exhibiting aspects of the behavior in question. Key words are the verbs or action phrases that best capture the essence of each behavior's dimensions. As an example, let's analyze the key words in the "Decisive Problem Solver" competency from the profile for the entry-level engineer we looked at in Chapter Four.

An entry-level engineer who is a decisive problem solver:

- Quickly obtains needed technical information from the most logical internal or external source when assigned an unfamiliar or challenging task
- Retains information and experience gained from the application of new information when solving a problem
- Detects deviations from standards by reviewing maintenance reports and probing for additional detail
- Projects the future impact of a current minor deviation and takes corrective action prior to problems becoming major difficulties
- Continuously reviews equipment and procedures, suggesting efficient changes to design and layout that cut down on working

distance, reduce mechanical failures, and result in improved workflow, lower production costs, better quality, and higher levels of safety

The key words from those behavioral statements are:

- Quickly obtains technical information
- Retains new information
- Detects deviations from standards
- Takes corrective action prior to problems becoming major difficulties
- Continuously reviews equipment and procedures

When the interviewer hears a key word, he or she should continue probing for additional details. Probing questions begin with: "Who," "Why," "When," "Where," and "How." "Why" questions are the most important to ask in order to get the candidate to reveal the information you need. Key words are a way to help you remember what you are looking for. They are your road map in the interview. However, candidates do not have to mirror these exact words in their responses.

Sample Behavioral Questions
Competency—Courage

Suggested Behavioral Questions

1. Tell us about a time when you spoke up about something you felt strongly about that others felt to be significantly wrong. Describe a time when you thought about speaking out but felt it best not to (contrary evidence).

   Then probe: At what point did you realize that others had a strong and different opinion? What steps did you take to deal with this situation? Who did you talk to? What was their response? What was the final outcome? Do you feel there is a certain situation within which you tend to "speak out?" If so, describe it. What can you do to prevent yourself from falling into this undesirable pattern in the future? What was the benefit to you for speaking out? What feedback did you get?

2. Tell us about a recent time when you were under a great deal of pressure to deliver on time.

    Then probe: Describe the situation in detail. What did you do to get the work done on time? What were the possible consequences you were concerned about? What was the outcome? If you were faced with a similar situation in the future, would you deal with it in the same way or differently? Why?

3. Describe a time when you recently took what you believed to be a significant risk. Describe a time when you felt you should have done something which others considered risky and consequently you didn't do it.

    Then probe: What was this risk? What about the risk made you feel comfortable taking it? Do you feel you made the right decision? What other risks have you taken and what have you learned from them? What feedback did you get from others? In retrospect, what would you do differently?

Competency—Responsibility

Suggested Behavioral Questions

1. Tell us about a time you were particularly proud of your decision.

    Then probe: What steps did you take in order to make this decision? What were some of the challenges you faced? Why are you particularly proud of this decision? What was the outcome? In retrospect, when could you have taken action to improve company performance and did not?

2. Describe a time when you had to choose between product delivery and quality.

   Then probe: Describe the situation in detail. What were some of the obstacles you encountered when attempting to get the work done? How did you deal with these obstacles? When you had ultimately finished the work how did you feel? What was the final outcome? What did you learn from this situation? What feedback did you get from others? What were the consequences?

3. Describe how you overcame an obstacle you considered significant in your life. Describe how you lived up to a commitment.

   Then probe: What obstacles did you encounter? How did you overcome these obstacles? Do you feel your persistence paid off? What, if anything, should you have done differently? What advice would you give young people looking for guidance to help them meet their personal and/or professional goals? What feedback did you receive from others?

Competency—Trust

Suggested Behavioral Questions

1. Describe the most significant effort you put in recently to live up to a difficult commitment.

   Then probe: Who else was involved? What steps did you take to live up to the commitment? What obstacles did you encounter? What was the outcome of the effort and meeting the commitment? What feedback did you get? How did you feel?

2. Describe a time when others around you seemed to work just to get by.

Then probe: What was distracting people from working harder? What was the level of cooperation and communication between people? How did you first recognize that people weren't giving their "all"? What did you do to increase communication? What effort was made to resolve conflict? Who initiated the resolution of conflict? How did they do it? What was the outcome? What feedback did you receive?

3. Describe a time when loyalty paid off for you.

Then probe: What do you feel was the driving force to maintain the loyalty? Why was this an effort? How did it pay off for you? What did other say or do in light of your commitment? What did you do to build the loyalty of others in the situation?

The Interview Guide

The interview guide contains all the information required for a hiring manager to conduct a successful behavioral interview. This includes the behavioral profile, a selection of behavioral questions, possible probing questions, and a list of key words that break down the profile into its essential indicators, space for taking notes based on the candidate's replies, and a system for rating answers and determining the candidate's fit for the job and the organization.

For HR leaders of the development process, the interview guide is an end product summarizing the energy put into the development of success profiles. It is also a means of communicating to the organization the information you've unearthed and refined. And finally, it is a reference to be used by each hiring manager in order to conduct a valid, accurate, and legally defensible interview consistent with other managers across the organization.

In most organizations, the interview guide becomes the record and proof that an interview was conducted in the best possible way. It can be referred to by anyone whether when analyzing candidates in large numbers or answering questions about selection decisions for or against a particular candidate.

But an interview guide is not just a safeguard or another form to be filled out to ensure compliability. It is, in fact, a tool that hiring managers quickly come to rely on and expect. By providing them with this tool soon after their training in behavioral interviewing, you give hiring managers all the information they need to make selection decisions that dramatically improve performance. The effectiveness of this interview guide is underlined by the case study profile below.

Sprint Canada

Victoria emphasizes how important a good interview guide was for the success of the process. "We developed a behavioral interviewing guide for each job." The hiring manager would receive their interview kit after training. The guide included the background for behavioral interviewing, "why it works better than other techniques, what makes it great, how to do it," then the interview guide was also provided on-line for all job families and all success profiles.

"Say you're interviewing for a cost accountant. You could read about what the success behaviors are for that kind of position and then read through the interview questions. The interview guide would mirror all the key behaviors and would have a selection of questions around each key behavior. As a hiring manager, all you would need to do is pick one or two questions from each key behavior and you've got your interview done.

"The good thing was people asked for it. They'd say, 'I was doing this and I have this whole new group of employees and I don't have a success profile or I don't have an interview guide.'" As with anything, the proof of a behavioral interviewing system's usefulness is whether it is being relied on by those responsible for the success of the new approach.

Summary

In order to conduct an effective interview, behavioral profiles must be translated into behavioral questions. As the example interview showed, behavioral questions are qualitatively different from traditional questions. Rather than focus on generalities that can be interpreted almost randomly, they probe for specific concrete examples of relevant experience. Because of this, the information that is gathered is considered to be high yield. Key words, siphoned from the profile itself, provide the interviewer with a signal that important information is being revealed. The interview guide reinforces the process and supports the ability of the interviewer to conduct the interview in an objective, thorough manner.

CHAPTER 6

Interviewing to Select and Sell the Best

Laying the Groundwork

Not every candidate from whom you receive a résumé will qualify for an interview. After you have screened the résumés to determine those who match your technical knock-out factors and have experiences that indicate a likelihood of opportunity to display the desired behaviors, you can invite them in for a behavioral interview. It's a lengthy and detailed process that should only be undertaken with those applicants who meet your base requirements or must-have competencies. Once the list of suitable applicants has been narrowed down, the hiring manager is ready to dig into the core behavioral issues that will determine which, if any, of the remaining candidates are a good fit for the job and the organization.

In traditional interviews the work might have started with the interview itself. In behavioral interviews the moment when candidate and hiring manager meet has been shored up and made meaningful by the way the fundamentals have been developed in advance. The job itself has been defined by an accurate job profile that reflects, in behavioral competency terms, the values unique to the organization. The interview guide has been prepared and serves the hiring manager as the hands-on tool for gathering essential information and ultimately making the best selection decision. It includes the must-have and preferred competencies, the key words that should be listened for, a list of behavioral questions that focus around the key behavioral competencies, and a systematic means of rating the answers.

How Much Structure?

Your goal is to select the candidate with the best fit. Most experienced hiring managers are well aware of the dangers of hiring in their own image. Though it would seem that an interview is the time to rely on the sharpness of our instincts and people skills, it is not. Personal biases and subjective judgments cloud the decision-making process. As much as possible, it is necessary to remove likes and dislikes, hot buttons and turn-offs from the gathering and analysis of information.

A solid job profile and the structured nature of the behavioral interview itself dramatically increase your ability to focus on the candidate's defining characteristics rather than on less relevant aspects to which you may find yourself drawn. To say that the behavioral interview is structured, however, should not imply that it is inflexible. In most cases, the interview guide will include three or more questions per behavioral competency, carefully written so that they seek the same data. This allows each interviewer to choose one question or more until the desired information is obtained. This also provides for an important sense of consistency and progress between interviews, if a round of interviews has been scheduled. Another interviewer, reviewing your notes and data, will be able to choose the next question on the list and obtain supporting or contrary information, thus furthering the organization's understanding of the candidate's suitability.

The essential reason for asking candidates the same questions is to ensure that the interviewers compare candidates against the profile rather than against each other. Without structure to the interview, hiring managers can "wander" in their questions, asking each candidate about related but ultimately different points. Although this may feel like a reasonable way of adapting to the nuances that each candidate brings to the table, it is a flood-gate for the biases and judgments that reduce the validity of the interview. An interviewer will project his or her own profile onto the candidate he or she likes; similarly, a candidate with high emotional intelligence will be able to read into an interviewer's likes and dislikes and tailor his or her image. Only a comparison of the candidate to the desired profile allows you to select the individual who is right for the job. This is achieved by identifying the degree of match between the job's requirements, the organization's values, and the individual's capabilities.

Some hiring managers are initially concerned by the structured approach. On the surface it can relay the impression that the process is robotic and clinical, yet nothing could be further from the truth. Yes, the same questions are meant to be asked of each candidate, but the dialogue that ensues is dynamic, engaging, and packed with valuable information. Because the questions are well thought out, the candidate is able to respond with meaningful information. During the interview process, stories emerge as do values and the things that motivate us. It can be very exhilarating for a candidate to open up about what moves him or her as a person and as an employee. Rather than being restrictive, the structured nature of a behavioral interview allows the interviewer and candidate the freedom to discuss what really matters. Think about the traditional interview to gain a picture of what it means to just go through the motions; despite the semblance of spontaneity and flexibility, the questions and the answers can often be predicted in advance.

The behavioral interview is, in fact, a fluid process involving much probing, give and take, follow-up, and the seeking of additional evidence for or against a particular behavior. This is not an easy thing to do well. Conducting a behavioral interview is a skill that starts with training and grows with experience. The questions are tools for digging out as much relevant factual information as possible.

HR must help develop the hiring manager into a skilled user of those tools. Since the job profile depicts exactly what it takes to be a top performer, HR must also hold the hiring manager accountable and responsible for the success, or failure, of the individual hired. In order to engage the hiring manager in understanding the importance of the behavioral profile and behavioral interviewing, it is recommended that hiring managers are trained in an experiential interactive workshop that enables them both to practice conducting an interview as well as to experience being behaviorally interviewed.

Time Allocation

The average traditional interview takes between 30 and 50 minutes. The bulk of that time, however, is meaningless since, as we've already discussed, the gut-hiring decision is actually made almost immediately at the outset of the interview. The behavioral interview requires that all judgments are suspended until after the interview is completed. At that time, the hiring manager can take a measured look at the collected data and compare it against the job profile. Because data collection is so important, the process takes considerably longer than both interviewer and candidate are used to. This should not be seen as an inordinate use of time but as an opportunity.

The behavior-based interview takes between 60 and 90 minutes, depending on the ability of the candidate to give quality behavioral answers and the ability of the interviewer to probe for additional information. For those who are impatient, this can seem like too much time. Yet compared to the months wasted if the wrong candidate is hired, it does not seem so long. The consequence of making a bad hire, based on a bad interview, is hours spent with the employee on correcting inappropriate on-the-job behavior. If you could avoid that by discovering the potentially poor fit during the interview, you will save considerable time in performance management conversations. Still, difficulty with the lengthy duration of behavior-based interviews is one of the reasons they fail.

The following is a snapshot of how time is allocated during a typical behavioral interview. If the interview takes one hour, then introductions should take five percent of the entire time, or around three minutes. Uncovering background information about the candidate accounts for 20 percent of the time, or 12 minutes. The portion of the interview dealing with the skills, knowledge, activities and experiences of the candidate as well as the behaviors involved should amount to 60 percent of the time, or around 36 minutes. Fifteen percent of the time, or around nine minutes, should be spent on closing and selling statements.

How Many Interviewers?

Some organizations rely on only one interviewer; others lean towards two or even a panel. Behavioral interviewing is flexible enough to adapt to any approach and will uncover high-quality information no matter what choice is made, but there are considerations to be made based on the skill of the interviewer.

Having only one interviewer requires a high degree of alertness and concentration in order to simultaneously ask questions, probe responses, and take notes as the interview progresses. Taking good notes while conducting questioning and probing presents a challenge, especially when first using behavioral techniques. You may miss key details.

Having multiple interviewers in the same interview has the advantage of efficiently focusing your assessment of applicant answers on critical points. When two or more interviewers are used, notes can be recorded more easily by assigning the interviewer and note taker roles. This frees the interviewer to probe, while the note taker concentrates on the responses. Although some candidates may find the presence of an additional note taker to be intimidating, in general, reactions have been positive. Assigning two interviewers in the interview with clear roles enhances the efficiency and effectiveness of the process. Post interview, most candidates provide the feedback that they were not intimidated and, in fact, appreciated the in-depth dialogue and comprehensive note taking.

Although not profiled in this book, Velcro Canada, another organization using behavioral interviewing, uses one interviewer for the first round of interviews and follows that with a panel process for the second round. Candidates debriefed after that second round positively noted that the questions between interviews were consistent and related and that, overall, there was a pattern to the interviewing process that made sense. Further, there was an advantage, in that once on the job, successful candidates already knew four people in the company who aided in their entry into the new organization.

Note Taking: Recording Behavioral Information

Since behavioral questions generate so many specific details, you need some way to recall them in order to make a measured judgment of the candidate after the interview. All questions will potentially provide information on myriad competencies. As a result, you need to wait until the end of the interview to provide an assessment of the candidate's articulated behaviors in comparison to the profile. Because of this, your ability to take notes becomes critical in assessing the candidate. You may also need to either defend or modify your ratings later on. In such cases, your notes are the only way you can back up or evaluate your decision.

It takes practice to learn how to accurately record key responses without distracting yourself or the candidate during the interview. Usually interviewers will have copies of the resumes or applications available at the interview for easy reference or to use as the basis of opening interview questions. Résumés are also referred to as a means of seeking out experiences that focus the behavioral discussion. When many applicants are being interviewed, interviewers often make notes on résumés in order to help differentiate candidates.

First, write the name of the interviewee, the date of the interview, and the name of the interviewers on the résumé or interview guide. Also, give yourself visual clues to the behavioral profile by writing the key words next to each question.

Throughout the interview, write the candidate's description of the critical incident being described, recording as many details that support the behavioral dimensions as you are assessing. Concentrate on the behaviors in question. Get the facts. Who was involved? When did it happen? What steps were taken? Where? Why? You should use the candidate's own words and avoid writing judgmental comments or your own view of their actions. Your opinions may not be an accurate reflection of the behaviors involved and may color a judgment best left until after the interview.

Once the interview is over and the candidate has left, you should review your notes and fill in any details you may have not written down. Do it when it is still fresh in your memory, preferably before your next interview.

Taking notes is a widely accepted part of most interviews that are conducted these days. As researcher Jennifer Burnett said in her article, "It is assumed that note taking results in more accurate recalls."[1] Burnett concludes that note taking has an impact on the validity of the selection, and furthermore, that recording behavioral information (as opposed to dispositional, contextual, procedural, or judgmental information) leads to the greatest level of validity.

Even though these notes may be solely for the use of the interviewer, if they identify or differentiate candidates by one of the criteria of the prohibited grounds—for example, "white female, 45ish," or "East Indian man, very pleasant"—they may be seen as evidence of intent to discriminate and could be used to try and prove bias in a human rights complaint. If you have any concerns or questions about human rights or the interviewing process you should consult your HR manager for clarification.

Some, though not many interviewers, like to video- or tape-record interviews, but I do not recommend this. Good behavioral note taking records sufficient quality information to make a valid decision. On top of this, video- or tape-recording can distract the candidate and make him or her nervous. There is no reason to add

---

[1] Jennifer R. Burnett, Chence Fan and Stephen J. Motowidlo, "Interview Notes and Validity," *Personnel Psychology*, (1998): 51.

stress to an already stressful situation. Again, it's important to be mindful of the intent to discriminate since legislation may prevent having a photo of a candidate prior to the candidate accepting the offer. If you have questions about your organization's use of photos or recordings in the selection process, consult HR or a labor or employment lawyer.

Preparing for the Interview

Although asking questions is the most critical skill for effective interviewing, there are other important considerations that are also important. How the interviewer conducts him- or herself, how the organization appears and how prepared the interviewer is, all influence the way the interview will go and affect the ultimate outcome. In addition, a strong candidate will be more apt to want to join an impressive organization that conducts a solid behavioral interview.

Your first responsibility is to know as much as possible about the job and the candidate before conducting the interview. Being a supervisor or manager of the position is not enough. You should have a solid understanding of the job's behavioral profile and all aspects of the interview guide. The candidate's written material might include an application form or résumé, perhaps a copy of a transcript or even results of tests or notes from a previous initial screening interview. These should all be reviewed thoroughly in advance and analyzed with the competency profile in mind and matched against the competency profile for the new position. Knowledge of them will be helpful in connecting with the candidate and he or she might provide clues as to what kinds of critical incidents will be uncovered.

As one of the first representatives of the organization to greet the applicant, your appearance is important. It should be appropriate to the company's image and to your particular position.

Likewise, the physical layout of the interview is important. What will be required? You'll need a table large enough for you and the candidate to have a common connection. If this is not possible, do not sit behind a desk as this will create a barrier. You should face the candidate on the same side of the desk and leave a space to take notes.

If there are several interviewers present, decide who will ask questions and who will take notes. Make arrangements not to be disturbed during the interview. The phone should be put on forward, the door closed against impromptu visitors. Even though a casual interruption might seem harmless to you, it can imply to the candidate that you don't take the interview or the candidate seriously—a possible sign of things to come, should the candidate come on board. If you have a screen saver on the computer or a sound signal when you receive e-mail, you should turn them off. Both can be annoying and distracting for someone unaccustomed to them. You want the candidate to be comfortable. When people are comfortable, they tend to relax and talk more freely.

Before the Interview

- Decide who will interview the candidate
- Divide the "must-have" behavioral and technical skills and knowledge
- Review the candidate's résumé so that you are familiar with the candidate's name, employment history, etc.
- Review the Behavioral Job Profile applicable to the vacancy and create behavioral questions that capture the "must-have's"
- Plan your time and divide the interview into segments:
    1. establishing rapport 5 percent
    2. background information and covering résumé 20 percent
    3. knowledge and behaviour questions 60 percent
    4. candidate's questions and close 15 percent

Opening the Interview

The first few minutes of the interview are important. What we do even in that short period of time can be critical to the success of the interview. Your initial objective is to put the candidate at ease so that quality information can be effectively exchanged. Balance warmth, friendliness, and empathy on the one hand with an objective, business-like task orientation on the other.

Your first moments of exchange will encourage or discourage rapport. When greeting the applicant, use a firm handshake and a sincere friendly smile. Establish appropriate eye contact and otherwise show that you are taking the time to make the candidate feel welcome and appreciated. Acting disorganized or harried, or otherwise indicating that this is an interruption in your full schedule, will turn off a candidate who expects your undivided attention.

There are ways that body language shows engagement. During exchanges, indicate you are listening by nodding your head. Vary your posture and body position from time to time, positively mirroring the candidate's physical position, if possible. When speaking, use a tone of voice that reflects your interest in what the candidate is saying as well as your own warmth and sincerity.

Two minutes, at most, of small talk is usually all that is required before an interview. You should include small talk as a way of establishing rapport and relaxing the candidate as well as getting a feel for how he or she communicates or comes across. Is the candidate a talker? Is he or she shy or reticent, calm, or nervous? All of these factors will influence how the interview is conducted and how probing questions will be used later.

When engaging in small talk, you should avoid topics that may not be of interest or might be inappropriate. Not everyone likes football or politics. Beginning a discussion on Monday night's game is liable to make the candidate feel awkward and uncomfortable if he or she watched something else. In general, small talk should avoid stressful topics. Safe topics might include how the candidate got to the interview, from what direction, whether he or she was able to find parking, if it was his or her first visit to the area, and so on.

The Agenda-Setting Statement

The purpose of the agenda-setting statement is to establish the tone of the interview and take control of the process. It includes a personal introduction, a description of the position, and an outline of the structure of the interview. It is important to be aware that not many people will be familiar with the behavioral interview. You will need to give the candidate a clear idea of what to expect.

In your introduction, you should make a brief description of your experience, background, and role in the organization, including, if you have not already done so, your name and title. You should also briefly detail the position, title, and department for which the candidate is being interviewed.

The candidate has probably been made aware of the amount of time the interview will take; nevertheless, you should give a brief breakdown of that time frame and describe what you want to accomplish. Is a decision going to happen at the end of the process or will further interviews be required? How long is the position being interviewed for?

You should mention that you will be taking notes during the interview. Some candidates may even feel unnerved by the interviewer writing while they talk, but they should understand that it is a part of the process. Though most people expect a certain amount of note taking, the detailed nature of behavioral notes may be a surprise. You should make the candidate aware that when his or her references are called, they will be asked behavioral questions as well. These questions will probably relate to specific things, such as critical incidents that have come up during the course of the interview. They will not involve judgments about character or ability.

For many people, behavioral questions will be considerably outside the range of what they have come to expect in an interview. It may even be unnerving for a candidate to know that the types of questions he or she has, no doubt, spent time preparing answers for, will not be of use. Explain that a behavioral interview examines what he or she has done in certain key situations in his or her work or life, in order to get insight into how he or she will perform on the job. The organization is using the technique because it generates higher quality information, allowing the selection of people who really fit the organization. Consequently, behavioral interviews are of benefit to the candidate as much as they are to the company, because they ensure that the best match will be made. You should put the candidate at ease by explaining that since the questions are, in fact, based on the things he or she knows best—his or her own experiences—they will be easier to answer than traditional questions. There are no judgments involved, no right or wrong answers—only experiences from which to draw inferences. Finally, the candidate should be made aware that he or she will be offered an opportunity to ask questions at the end of the interview.

I suggest that you spend a good deal of time thinking about formulating an agenda-setting statement. It will help to write down your statement and memorize it in order to lead into the interview most efficiently. The following sample will give you an idea of how to proceed, but you will need to tailor yours to suit your needs:

Sample Agenda-Setting Statement

To help us identify the very best candidates for this position, it's important for us to learn "how" you approach your work. This will help us determine your suitability for this position at this time.

We are now going to ask you two types of questions. The first set of questions is of the more traditional nature. The second set of questions asks you to describe examples of incidents from your own personal experience. The more specific you can make your stories, the better an appreciation we will get of your capabilities. We are particularly interested in what you did (or how you acted) in these incidents. We might interrupt you now and then to remind you to stay focused in each case on your personal contribution rather than on what the team or a colleague might have done. We might also ask for references of other people, not just your manager, who were involved in the incidents you share with us.

We will be taking notes during the process of the interview. We take notes to ensure that we can differentiate between our candidates and be more objective about differentiating their answers. We expect that this interview will take approximately one-and-a-half hours.

It may take you some time to think of an appropriate example when we ask you to describe a situation. Don't worry if it does. Take your time and think of your response before providing an answer. We also want to provide you with an opportunity to ask questions. We will review any questions you might have at the end of this process.

Let's begin.

After the agenda-setting statement the interviewer asks the opening question.

Open-Ended and Closed-Ended Questions

Both open-ended and closed-ended questions have their place in an interview. Since they generate different kinds of answers, you should be aware of when and how to use them skillfully.

An open-ended question is structured to encourage candidates to respond in detail. It is particularly useful when looking for behavioral information, since we want the candidate to be expansive about a situation he or she was involved in. The more information the candidate reveals, the clearer the understanding the interviewer will have of that person's behavior.

Open-ended questions begin with such phrases as, "Tell me about the time when...," "What was your most..." or "Give me an example of...."—they encourage the candidate to talk. Typically, answers to open-ended questions will begin like stories with phrases like, "When I was...," "While a manager of distribution I..." or "After graduation I...." Such answers lend themselves to details about situations in which past performance or actions can be judged.

Close-ended or direct questions encourage only "yes" or "no" answers. Specific detailed information about past behavior is obviously much more useful than a string of "yes" and "no" answers. But close-ended or direct questions have their uses. They can be applied at the start of the interview to build rapport and put the candidate at ease. They can also be appropriate for confirming concrete details on a resume or application. And they can serve to clarify behavioral information once the candidate has described a critical incident. Examples of this latter usage might include, "So, your role was to supervise the team?" "Was the proposal approved?" or "Did you accept the transfer?"

It is only when closed-ended questions are used unskillfully that there is trouble. Asking, "Are you attentive to detail?," "Do you like working with people?" or "Are you a team player?" and expecting behavioral information is a mistake. The candidate's only possible answer is "yes" or "no." If the candidate senses that you are looking for more, he or she might continue to expand on that "yes" or "no," but it is unlikely that you are going to get at quality behavioral data that way. Also people expect that if you describe your organization as a team and people environment that they must answer "yes." They then feel the need to proceed with generic yet enthusiastic responses as to why. The reality may be that they love working with people, but are not successful at it!

Another frequent questioning mistake is to telegraph an answer. If an interviewer says, "We're looking for people who delegate well. As a manager, how do you delegate?" the candidate understands that he or she better answer in a particular way or risk getting the question wrong. This tells the candidate exactly what is the desired answer; it is not a behavioral question.

Listening

By asking behavioral questions, you are trying to prompt the candidate to think of specific incidents in his or her past that have a bearing on the behavioral competencies of the position. If the candidate is able to think of an experience, the interviewer listens and takes notes and only asks further questions about that experience in order to understand the critical incident, the outcome, and the underlying behaviors involved. Good interviewing is 85 percent listening. Probing questions are used sparingly to prompt the candidate to open up and reveal essential details.

Remember that a behavioral interview is a new experience for most candidates. Thinking of actual experiences takes time and energy. Sometimes the candidate might not have had the kind of experience you are searching for. Sometimes the candidate may have difficulty thinking of the "best" experience to relate. For many people, talking so descriptively about themselves may not be what they expected or what they are used to.

During the introduction, the interviewer must let the candidate know that it is quite acceptable to take a few minutes to think of examples. Most of us are uncomfortable when it comes to silent situations. If you told the candidate that he or she has a few minutes, do not interrupt after a few seconds.

As interviewer, you must practice patience and be comfortable with silences. In fact, one of the most effective techniques of behavioral interviewing is silence. It allows the candidate time to think and prompts him or her towards specific examples to break the silence. Since most of us are uncomfortable with silence, it is difficult to let the time pass. We are eager to fill the void in an uncomfortable pause. But it takes time to think of an example to answer a behavioral question. You need to let the candidate know that silence is acceptable by not filling in the gap with more talk.

When the candidate pauses before answering a question, wait 10 to 15 seconds before interrupting. This is not an easy thing to do. Try timing yourself for 15 seconds and you will be surprised at how long the duration seems. But get used to that kind of gap and be practiced in letting it expire. At the end of 10 to 15 seconds, reassure a candidate through supportive non-verbal as well as verbal messages. Comfortable body language speaks volumes and may be sufficient. If you sense that the candidate is concerned about the amount of time passing to the point that he or she feels an answer is in jeopardy, reassure him or her. Say something like, "I realize that it can be difficult to dig up some of these past examples. Most people have to take time to do so. That's okay, because the responses are very helpful."

If the candidate is still unable to come up with an answer, then it may be time to restate the question using different words. For instance, if the initial question "Describe a recent incident when you were able to help a co-worker solve a difficult problem" is met with silence, you may wish to rephrase the question by asking, "Describe a time, either at work or at school, when you provided information others needed to solve a problem." Conversely, you may wish to broaden the range of experience that you are seeking.

When the candidate begins to speak, it is necessary to practice good listening habits. Be genuinely interested in what the person is saying. Paraphrase often to show that you understand or to give the candidate a chance to correct any misperceptions. Taking notes also indicates you are listening, but it is important not to forget that you are in close proximity to the candidate. Don't bury yourself in your notepad; look up occasionally, nod or give other signs that you are taking the information in and following the story.

Probing

Our experience has shown that the more skilled an interviewer is in asking behavioral questions, the more relevant information he or she gathers from the interviewees. It is important that an interviewer learn how to probe effectively in order to gather all the relevant information from the candidate. Once you have asked your opening question, follow up with additional questions to gather details. Skilled probing requires that the interviewer pay close attention to the candidate's responses.

You should probe until you understand the critical incident, the underlying behaviors, and the outcome. Think of the journalist who goes after a story by asking "how, what, when, where, and why." Conduct your interview like a root cause analysis. Ask "why" about one critical incident up to five times. By the fourth or fifth time, you'll know more about the candidate's behavior than they'll ever want to tell you.

You need detail. The purpose of your probing is to validate the candidate's behaviors against the job profile. But you should not try to force-fit those behaviors. Some of us have a tendency to find what we are looking for. For this reason, I strongly suggest that you actively seek out contrary evidence in order to verify whether a behavior has really been exhibited or not. Ask the candidate to describe a time when he or she didn't respond in that way. Use the rule of three: always seek three examples of every behavior you aim to identify by probing three different incidents at three different times. Otherwise, you will be hearing only about one, or possibly two stories, from multiple perspectives throughout the interview.

You should also probe to understand the parameters of the critical incident. For example, it is important to gather evidence regarding the time frame of the situation to confirm the consistency of demonstrating the behaviors. You will know that the candidate has provided you with enough information when you can see the event unfold in your mind like a scene from a movie.

Here are some sample questions and the probing questions used in follow-up:

Question:	*Being able to respond to a customer's concern is important in the job of a computer scientist. Yet not all customers are alike and not all are nice or easy to understand. Describe a time when you were working with a customer who was either not cooperative or not clear in what he or she wanted. What was the situation? How did you proceed to work with the person to satisfy his or her real needs?*
Probing:	*What did you do? How did you achieve understanding? What was the customer's reaction? What were the consequences or outcomes?*
Question:	*Getting support and resources for a project is essential to your success. Describe a time when you were successful in getting buy-in from people in other functions or teams and you were able to get them to lend you resources.*
Probing:	*What did you do? How did you overcome resistance? What were the consequences? How often does this happen?*
Question:	*Important to the position of a computer scientist is the ability to learn new information and continuously improve his or her knowledge of the product the*

> *company offers. Describe how you go about learning new information that is important to your job and to the department.*
>
> **Probing:**   *How often do you do this? What was the last relevant book you read? What have you done in terms of personal development?*

Probing questions allow the interviewer to break free from the set questions that must be asked of every candidate. They allow the interviewer to dig deeper in a disciplined fashion. The goal is to probe for actual behaviors. If the candidate's answers are not what you need for sufficient behavioral data, don't be afraid to take control of the interview.

Getting Behavioral Answers

It can be difficult to get behavioral information out of some candidates. Despite clearly explaining that what you are looking for are specific details related to the candidate's personal involvement in a past situation, some candidates will find ways to resist or avert a concrete answer.

Knowing in advance how candidates can typically evade a response helps in using counter-tactics to still hone in on relevant behavioral information. In all, there are three general approaches to spot:

1. Candidates who claim either not to have had such an experience at all or for whom the experience is "so common" that no specific examples come to mind.

2. Candidates who refuse to link their answer to a concrete time but instead give a theoretical response.

3. Candidates who deliberately make their role in a group effort unclear.

It is your responsibility to overcome these obstacles in the interview and reorient the questions to obtain good data. Here are some sample difficulties and suggested responses.

Candidates Who Deny the Experience

Question: *Tell me about a time when you were involved in a dispute with a customer.*

Answer: *I'm not sure if I've ever had such an experience.*

How do you handle a situation in which a candidate insists that he or she has never had an experience like the one you are hoping to learn about? Some candidates will be frustratingly vague, claiming that they've never experienced a time when they were unable to deal with a customer's complaints or work through a problem. Others will claim that the experience is so frequent that no specific example comes to mind. They might say, "I just can't think of an example," or "That happened all the time at my job but I can't remember a particular time."

Patiently, the interviewer tries again. "I realize that it's difficult to come up with an example, but can you give it a try?" It may help to restate the question using different words. Or you may wish to broaden the field by inviting the candidate to think of any situation, even if it did not take place during his or her last job. Remember, give the candidate time to think and use the 15-second rule, even when restating a question. It may surprise you, but an answer almost always emerges.

Candidates Who Give Theoretical Responses

Question: *Tell me about a time in which you had to criticize an employee for a delay in handling a customer's concerns.*

Answer: *As a manager, that's always something I have in the back of my mind. As far as I'm concerned, whenever a customer sales rep is handling a problem, he or she should deal with it immediately and directly. Taking ownership is important. I tell people this all the time.*

Even when an answer is forthcoming, it can still be difficult at times to obtain behavioral data. Some candidates may try to give the appearance of supplying the information you seek, when in fact they have dodged the bullet.

Evasiveness is not difficult to spot. The candidate will give you what amounts to a typical way he or she would respond to a situation rather than an actual way. If the answer is not grounded in the past tense, then what he or she is describing is not a specific concrete event.

In order to get at a specific critical incident, probe for concrete details. Ask the candidate to describe a specific time when the critical incident happened. Find out what the customer's complaint, was, how the employee handled that complaint, and what specifically the manager did in critiquing the employee. What was the result of that action?

In a behavioral interview, we are not interested in theoretical answers but actual behaviors. It is easier to say what one would have done or would do, but a more accurate analysis of behavior is based on what one actually has done. Someone claiming, "Hard work is important to me and working long hours comes with the territory," does not tell you as much as someone who says, "The last two projects I had to work on involved weekends and evenings in order to meet our deadline." Likewise, "Customer service is my main priority as a clerk. I like to make people feel they are treated well," does not say as much as, "I always notice people's names on their credit cards and use them when I speak to them. Last week a man came in and I greeted him by name. He was so pleased."

Candidates Who Are Vague

Question: *Information Services has to respond to many sudden emergencies. Tell me about how you handled an emergency.*

Answer: *It's important to remain calm and deal with problems step by step. I remember once when the entire system crashed because of the Melissa Virus. No one in the organization knew what was going on. But those of us in IS handled it very coolly. We visited*

> *each workstation and got everyone out of their locked systems. We had to deal with a lot of concerned and angry people along the way, senior people with a lot of clout who were always blaming us when they had a problem and forgetting us when we solved it for them....*

Sometimes a response is detailed, but a candidate's role in those circumstances is vague and difficult to assess or analyze. That kind of an evasive answer is marked by the frequent use of the pronoun "we" instead of "I." The interviewer should probe to focus on the direct role or actions of the candidate. Too many people love to use "we." Break it down. Ask specifically, "What was your involvement?" Behavioral answers must be concrete and must focus on the individual involved.

When the candidate is having problems giving an answer, you will have problems gathering the kind of information that you need to make your selection decision. It's up to you to establish conditions which help the candidate recall past experiences. Take responsibility for not posing the question properly to get specific examples. Reassure the candidate. Restate the question using different words and try again. Stress that you're seeking a specific description of a situation. Rely on a calculated pause or a sympathetic but persistent approach to coax a better answer. Clarify the behavior you are seeking. With these methods you can nail down what that person will do during a real critical incident that pertains to the behaviors that your organization needs.

Selling Your Organization

When a behavioral interview is drawing to a close, it is necessary to review notes and score answers before an accurate selection decision can be made. Nevertheless, the quality and aptness of the behavioral information you have unearthed should provide you with enough guidance to determine whether you should end the interview without fanfare or seize the opportunity to lay out a compelling argument for your organization.

A behavioral interview is, in and of itself, an outstanding selling tool. Candidates who have experienced them invariably say that they understand the organization's needs, values, and direction in very concrete terms. Perhaps even more importantly, those candidates also feel that the organization now understands important information about them, their goals, and values, their motivators and means of getting the job done. This results in a certain amount of self-selection. When an individual becomes aware that he or she is a good fit for an organization and a particular position, it's a powerful and compelling emotional argument to join your organization. This can be a particularly helpful differentiator with members of Generation X. More so than those from other demographic groups, members of Generation X exercise their need to be recognized for their individual qualities and to identify strongly with the organization for which they will ply their best efforts. Experiencing a behavioral interview can provide a compelling rationale for joining your organization over another.

Another important means of selling a candidate on your organization is telling the truth. The candidate has been concrete and honest with you; it's now time to return the courtesy. Describe the job and the organization in detail. Make sure the candidate understands the advantages and disadvantages the position presents. While you want to accentuate the positive, you should not brush under the rug the difficulties that the candidate might face if hired. A candid, open approach works better in the long run since it avoids unrealistic expectations on the part of new hires. List some key benefits and opportunities of the position for which you are interviewing the candidate. Then list the major challenges. Describe the organization's or the job's weak points. If promotions are slow or tasks are highly repetitive, say so. If upper management never has any time for regular meetings, be open about that. If the candidate knows what to expect, then he or she has a clearer understanding of the company's values. You want your new hires to be on your side from the beginning, reinforcing the organization's strengths and correcting its weaknesses without dragging everyone down with complaints about surprising aspects of this new culture.

Closing Interview Tips

- Thank the applicant for answering the questions and for his or her time commitment

- Provide an outside date by which the applicant should hear from the organization (don't commit to a specific time if you don't know)

- Inform the applicant of the expected time frame and sequence of next events before the hiring decision is made

- Double check the applicant's references provided during the interview

- Suggest to the candidate that he or she may call you, after the interview is over, if he or she recalls any information that might be useful to your decision-making process

- If you are interested in the candidate, then inquire about his or her interest in the position and availability (e.g., other job offers, how close to a decision he or she is, etc.). Be careful not to state or imply that you will be offering him or her the job

---

Closing the Interview

At the conclusion of the interview, wrap up with a statement that communicates your interest in the information you have gathered and inform the applicant of what happens next. Thank the applicant for answering the questions and for his or her time commitment. Provide an outside date by which the applicant should hear from your organization, but don't commit to a specific time if you don't know. Inform the applicant of the time frame and sequence of the decision-making process and review the name of the references that the candidate has provided.

Again, if you are interested in the candidate, check on his or her interest in the position along with his or her availability. Does he or she have other offers? How close is he or she to a decision? While you need to be measured and systematic in your rating of the candidate before you make a decision, you should also make sure you understand his or her situation; you don't want to lose out on someone who may be a top performer and your first choice.

Behavioral Reference Checks

Reference checks are important. First, it's important to validate that someone actually has the experience and credentials that you require. It's all too common today for job experience and even academic degrees to be exaggerated or even fabricated. Second, a behavioral reference check is a way of gaining another perspective on a candidate's on-the-job behaviors. It removes the subjective judgment or over-flattery typical of traditional reference checks and hones in on concrete actions.

A minimum of two, and preferably three, reference checks need to be completed to conclude the hiring process. They should be provided or obtained in good faith, employment-related, done in a timely fashion, focused on factual information, objective, job-specific, and conducted in a manner equitable to all candidates under final consideration.

During the interview, confirm with the candidate your interest in following up to validate or verify the information you've obtained. Ask for names of other people besides the candidate's manager. Try to get references specific to the most relevant of experiences discussed in the interview. If applicable, ask the candidate to sign an appropriate portion of the application, thus enabling you to pursue a reference from a particular individual. Suggest that the candidate contact his or her references first, so they know in advance who you are and why you are calling.

You need to maintain a written record of information obtained. It is also necessary to assess all information against the job profile and your interview notes and rating.

When calling, begin by identifying yourself and stating the reason for your call. Mention that you hope that the candidate called prior to your contacting the reference. If the person is skeptical, offer your number so the validity of the call can be confirmed, and suggest he or she call you back.

Start by verifying factual information, dates of employment, and job title. Be positive. Take specific incidents that you need verified or explained further from the actual interview. You should avoid opinion questions. For example, don't ask about the candidate's strengths and weaknesses or inquire as to whether the former employer would hire the person again. These questions are not specific to the position in your company.

Again, the rule of three should be in play. Select three behavioral questions to ask. Probe for the candidate's involvement in events specific to demonstrating a good fit at your company. If you do not focus on the behaviors the referee has observed, information will be hearsay and invalid.

Different people have different interpretations or standards as to what constitutes effective job performance. For that reason, don't get into judgments. Rather, focus on behavioral descriptions of critical incidents you learned about during the interview. For example, "Erin noted that while she was working with you, the level of client service in the area improved significantly. Please describe what happened to improve client service." Allow the person to describe what happened and probe for further behavioral details. Then, if the individual did not make specific reference to Erin's involvement and her relationship to the work, ask specifically what Erin's role was.

Listen actively on the phone. Be aware of hesitation in comments or groping for answers. Don't compare one candidate to another or one employee to another. What was excellent for the person on the phone might not be acceptable to your company. Remember, if the reference is from someone who has not worked with the candidate recently, the candidate's approaches and skill sets may have changed or grown over time.

If the reference voluntarily mentions that the person was fired, seek additional information. Summarize with an open-ended question such as "Is there anything you would like to add?" Finally, thank the person for his or her time.

Post-Interview Debriefings

Especially for internal competitions, candidates who were not selected for a position may ask to meet with you or another member of the selection team to understand why they were not chosen. The behavioral data you gathered in the interview allows you to do so in clear concrete terms, linked to job competencies, and organizational values. In this way you are able to give an objective, job-based rationale for why the candidate was not the best fit. You may even be able to provide developmental tips for how the candidate could succeed should they decide to reapply in the future. It is important, for these reasons, that you provide accurate feedback, with a positive intent.

Giving feedback is easier if during the interview process you took accurate notes of the candidate's answers. You should record the name of the candidate on the assessment form along with the names of the interviewers and the date of the interview. It will help if you have assessed the candidate immediately after the interview.

A post-interview can be an emotionally charged meeting. Usually when candidates have lost a competition, they go through a grieving period that can include shock, anger, rejection, acceptance, and a request for help. It is important that during the meeting you listen without interruption to the concerns of the candidate. Only once the candidate has had a chance to express his or her concerns or feelings, should you begin to go over their answers.

Remember to remain calm. Doing so will help you focus on giving the individual proper feedback. If you find the tension is high, excuse yourself and get a glass of water. Remember that you are in control.

A post-interview should be prepared for in the same way as the interview. You should ensure that there are no interruptions —and a table where you both can sit at equal stations. Be ready to stop the meeting if it gets out of control.

Remember that you have assessed the candidates based on their specific and individual responses and evaluated them in terms of this job's requirements. Do not specifically compare the candidate's answers with those of other candidates. As a closing statement, you may invite the candidate to consult with the HR staff.

Ensuring the Fit of Your Selection

Once you have identified the best candidates from your pool of applicants, there are ways in which you can gain further certainty of their fit.

Following the behavioral interview, I recommend conducting a situational interview with your finalists. A situational interview poses a hypothetical situation. The candidates are asked how they would respond in that situation. I recommend that you base the situational interview for finalists on an ethical dilemma that is currently being debated within the organization. In this way you can gain a deeper insight into each candidate's match with your organization's values. For example, your company is transitioning from rewarding individual contributions to rewarding teamwork. You might want to ask each finalist how he or she would make a decision on the allocation of a reward when it's commonly known that one individual has disproportionately contributed to the team's success. This exercise will allow you to assess each candidate's responses for consistency with the organization's values and behaviours.

Remember, congruity of the candidate's values and the organization's ensures long-term fit—especially during tough or highly competitive times. Such values can only be accurately observed in the candidates' behaviors. If you are looking for a person who will have a strong positive impact on your organization and stay for a sufficient period of time, there is no better measure. In particular, when interviewing candidates who are members of Generation X, you will be able to define what makes your organization a fun, satisfying or great place to work in concrete terms. "Fun" for some people is working on a project for long hours; "satisfying" might mean a good balance of personal life and work; the point is to discover whatever these elusive notions mean in your industry and to the candidate specifically.

It is also important to provide a realistic job preview for your finalists. Go deeper than you did during the interview. Tell them about opportunities as well as what is possibly wrong with the organization. Your candidness in combination with the behavioral interview will give the candidate a clear grasp of the organization and its values, goals, and environment. Contrary to what many might think, such a realistic snapshot of the candidate's possible future is a good thing. The exchange of information creates, on both sides, a sense of understanding, patience, respect, and excitement.

Training Hiring Managers to do Behavioural Interviewing

Here are some ideas that explain why training frontline managers is important. It is focused on providing them with the tools and process that enables them to become accountable and responsible for the hiring decision. It transfers to managers an in-depth understanding of how behaviours are an essential aspect of success in achieving the desired business results.

When I ask managers what are the three most difficult things they do, the universal answer is hiring, performance reviews (correcting poor performance), and firing. The process of teaching managers that behavioral interviewing will give them tools and process to take the mystery and the fear out of interviewing is like lifting a burden from them.

Training line managers in behavioral interviewing empowers managers to make correct decisions. It also removes the "blame human resources" attitude for bad selection decisions. As things currently stand, most managers do not feel accountable for hiring decisions. In fact, human resources is a convenient whipping post for nearly all bad people decisions and rarely gets the credit when people decisions turn out to be correct. Specifically, managers, when they realize that a new employee (even one they interviewed and selected) is not working out, are quick to complain that human resources "just doesn't understand the job" and therefore doesn't attract the right kind of person in the first place. If, by chance, the hire turns out to be the right one, managers typically credit their own gut-instincts for the success—a dubious standard at best.

For any organization's selection process to improve, it is important to turn this blame-game around by creating a culture in which managers are held accountable for all hiring decisions. This does not come about simply by supplying interview guides with ready-made behavioral profiles and questions. Managers need to buy into the power of behavioral profiles as a way of determining exactly what the job and organizational culture requires. They need to understand how radically different the quality of information obtained from behavioral questions is, as compared to traditional questions. And they need to see first-hand how a behavioral interview sets the tone for a future career with high performance standards and clear expectations.

There is only one way to communicate all this and more: through the education provided in the training process. It's an unprecedented opportunity to give managers, not only the tools and skills necessary to hire right, but also the enthusiasm and excitement about their ability to be objective and accurate in the hiring decision and responsible for its success.

Training takes a hiring manager through a journey that allows him or her to:

- Learn the overall process of the behavioral interview
- Recognize that behavioral information is the best kind of information for predicting future on-the-job success
- Participate in developing behavioral profiles for the jobs he or she is seeking to fill, or, if the profiles are already built, walk through a discussion of how those behaviors are indeed the ones that predict exceptional performance
- Understand how to build questions based on the profile that enables candidates to reveal their own behavioral competencies through stories about past experiences
- Experience how behavioral questions elicit superior information
- Practice how to probe, follow-up, listen, and other skills necessary for conducting the interview successfully

- Learn how to score answers effectively

- Understand the importance of withholding judgment and relating behavioral scores to the profile, in order to avoid comparing candidates to each other

- Sell the organization and the job to a candidate who fits the profile

Without exception, the case studies that follow show that managers who were educated thoroughly in behavioral interviewing experienced a nearly born-again reaction to their understanding of the power of behavioral questions to help select the right people. Empowering managers in this way is a selling tool in and of itself, a chance to make converts and fervent believers out of the people who are most responsible for and affected by the act of hiring in the organization.

Demonstrating the Power of Behavioral Questions

"What are your strengths and weaknesses?"

Few questions elicit less valuable information and yet are more universally employed. Managers need to be shown that there is a much better way.

To get their attention, demonstrate how useless a traditional question is in eliciting concrete, useful detail. Ask them to ask their own children, "What did you learn in school today?" As they probably already know, the nearly universal response is, "Nothing." Ask them to try another traditional question, "How was school today?" in follow-up. No doubt they know the answer to that one too: "Boring."

Now, get them to try a behavioral question. Using words and terms young people can relate to, tell them to ask their children, "What was the most frustrating thing that happened to you today?" Chances are the answer will be detailed, concrete, and extensive. Follow that one up with, "What was the most challenging thing you did today?" It's likely that the information elicited will help paint a better picture of what happened, how it was handled, and what resulted.

The result is a much more meaningful discussion in general. By changing to behaviour-focused—open-ended questions—the child is "forced" to reveal more of what happened at school and his or her feelings about school. Parents should be warned, however, that asking behavioral questions might force them, as well, to learn more about what's really going on than they are prepared for!

Case Study Profiles

All of the case studies we profiled for this book had very positive feedback from hiring managers about the new behavioral interviewing system. Although some people acknowledged that there were challenges in implementing the system, they were definitely worth it.

Abbott Labs

As Andrée Charbonneau of Abbott Labs says, "I can't think of a single manager who would revert back to a traditional interviewing approach. Now that they've been working with behavioral interviewing and with the competencies, they're taking that very seriously. The process of updating the competency profiles now comes directly from the managers. It's not HR prompting and saying, 'come on your profile is two years old now, maybe we should have a look.' People are taking the initiative and saying 'come on let's make sure it stays current.'"

For the actual interviews, Abbott Labs uses a mix of approaches. "Our hiring process at entry-level has three levels, so there are really three series of questions, all based on the behavioral profile." This provides for a sense of progression between interviews both for the candidate and the organization. "There's a series of questions for product management, with a different one for associate product or senior, depending on the depth. Most of them are behavioral, but not all of them. We do some situational questions and some paper exercises, depending on the job, so it's not exclusively behavioral."

Andrée found understanding the definition of the job profile's competency and how that translated into the interview questions was the most difficult thing. "I think the hardest part for a manager is not in switching to the old interview style but in figuring out what to do with the answer. You need to understand that yes, everyone will give you an answer, but how do you go to that answer and really figure out whether the candidate is really right for the job? That is where our redefinition of the competencies [from the off-the-shelf competency system to the internally developed system] helped a lot. It was easier to understand what it is that we're looking for. It helped the managers fish out of the very many answers they could get what it was that they were really after."

Michelin North America

Feedback at Michelin North America was also very positive. People doing the interviewing, "felt very very confident. Quite often the people who do the selection process are wondering 'how do I make judgments about people?' [Behavioral interviewing] gave them something concrete that was intuitively right, and it yielded better results."

Feedback from candidates was also strong. "People found that they respected the fact that there was a reasonable structure to the interview. It seemed logical and evident. Whenever a person came to visit one of our facilities for an interview, we explained that they would be meeting with a number of people, each person focusing on a different area, so it all seemed logical in approach. We got a lot of positive feedback because of that."

In actual rounds of interviewing, different interviewers took on specific roles. "Everyone that conducted part of the interview was trained and generally assigned one or two facets for each person. They would have sample questions and would concentrate in one specific area." For example, "I would work on two of the key behaviors and someone else would focus on a few others. Then we would meet at the end of the day and sort of exchange information.

"For most people the discipline was logical so [the interviewing process] was viewed as very helpful. I would have expected that some people would have felt constrained, but I never heard that feedback."

In particular, because of the nature of the candidates' probing and in-depth follow-up, questions came easily to the interviewers at Michelin. "We were talking very specifically to people coming out of universities. In most universities, in the fourth year of engineering, they do a project so you'd always be able to ask about the project. That work could be assessed from a technical point of view, but it also became a good focus for the teamwork aspect and understanding what role people played. It was a very natural kind of thing. You had people who had fairly similar kinds of experiences. The project lent itself well to that [kind of probing]."

When it came to scoring and consistency, training was important. During the two-day training program, Michelin would "quite often bring in candidates to interview so that people had a chance to do [live scoring]."

HMV Canada

At HMV Canada, training was also two days. "We did training workshops around the country on behavioral recruiting," Marnie Falkiner says. The training needed to be tailored for the audience of mostly young people. "We would have people with little education other than high school. They were visual and audio oriented. And we did a variety of activities within the training, including video and role playing."

As Marnie describes it, "because they are young, into music, and very social, they didn't like role playing at first. But when we actually got into it, they loved it. We would do it in front of them, then role play with them, then put them into groups so they would do it together with each other. We would ask for scenarios of different types of people they were encountering in interviews so that they could see what those types actually looked like in a behavioral interview. It allowed them to look at those people objectively, to determine what was a match and what wasn't a match, as well as how you draw that out in interviews."

The candidates themselves "are very young and have limited experience at being interviewed as well as limited life and work experience." The problem is, "How can you translate certain life experiences into the business world?" Behavioral interviews allow inferences to be made about non-work experiences as long as they display the desired behaviors. "So past behavior is an indication of future behavior. Otherwise, it's hard to interview really young people. It helped to understand how to translate behaviors."

Throughout the training workshops, Marnie "went through all questions and ended up with a series of best asked questions." She had already done workshops to gather information about what best activities were in hiring and she collected that "so that at the end of the training we were able to send a book out from things that they told us. We could say, 'These are the top five questions, and these are the kinds of answers you're looking for.' It always helped to say these are the questions, and these are what are you looking for in the answers."

Thomas Cook

In her original work at Thomas Cook, Christine Deputy also found that training for behavioral interviewing was made even more effective by using real candidates to get the message across. "When we did the behavioral interviewing training, we did a two-and-a-half day program using actual candidates who were interested in working with us. It was an incredibly powerful process, because what happens is you have one candidate interviewed by two different groups and then you get those groups, to compare their notes. Some of the feedback was, 'I would have hired this individual had I interviewed them my old way and now I would never hire him.' Or, 'I would never have hired this person before and now I'm really interested in her.' We really worked on first impressions with the interviewers.

"The other feedback we got was that it is amazing how easy the interview can be when you know what you're looking for. If you know what the right answer is, it's really something how consistent you can be with your peers on how you score a candidate."

Christine has some insights into the psychology of the interview process as to why this is so. "A lot of that is because when we interview, we're listening for something, but what I might be listening for and what you might be listening for are possibly two different things. A lot of it has to do with communication styles. If I give you information in a way that you don't like to get it, say you're more fact-driven, more information-focused, and I'm very expressive and very emotive, I might be talking about dreams and excitement and future, and you might think that's all fluff. On the other hand, someone else hearing that might think, 'Well that's exactly what I want.' So the question is, what's the right answer? We don't all have the right answer, but there is one right answer defined by the right behaviors. It's a hard thing to teach to HR people, I find. They want to be able to give somebody credit for a good answer..." and hope that the candidate can develop the necessary behaviors once on the job. As Christine puts it, however, "We don't have the opportunity in business today to hope that someone will turn out. You need to hire for the right set of behaviors from the beginning."

Starbucks

Another interesting positive reaction to the use of behavioral interviewing is how it promotes diversity in the organization's workforce. At Starbucks, Christine says, diversity is "one of our core values." And diversity is not only about racial issues; it's "also about approach and communication styles. The great thing about behavioral interviewing is that if you use it well, it will help you build a diverse workforce because it forces you to listen to answers as opposed to evaluating style and presentation. We're such creatures of our own personal styles that we have a hard time letting go and not reacting on our own preferences."

Christine says, "One of the hardest things is the structure." Most people resist the structure. It takes a while to get to the level of skill where you can interview someone and not have to just read each question, finish the question, and go on to the next one.

"You have to be good at doing that. You have to commit for a while and say, 'Why don't you take me through your resume and tell me what you did at those different jobs?' And then, 'Well you know at that job, you were working with a team, can you tell me a specific example where there was a lot of conflict? You can then integrate their experience into questions with a more conversational tone and make it smooth. Up to that point, you need to be pretty strict about asking the behavioral questions and being a strong listener. People think it's easy, but you really have to work at it and that's a hard thing to teach. And it's a hard thing to learn."

Other obstacles Christine has found with behavioral interviewing have to do with time, in particular, both the time needed for adequate training and the time needed for the interview itself. At Starbucks, "I can't spend two-and-a-half days training store managers on how to do interviews. You have to make your choices. I have a day and a half to do upskilling with our district managers, and then I have to give them a process they can use pretty easily without a lot of error.

"The interview itself also takes longer. I can't do it in less than two hours. You need that much time to really understand someone. You need to allow the candidate to explore the concepts and get all the information and the contrary evidence. There's a lot of resistance to that, because we are a society that likes to do things quickly."

Nevertheless, Christine says, "The interview is only as good as you are. If you don't get the information, the responsibility is yours, not the candidate's."

Calgary Police Service

Dale Burns of the Calgary Police Service praises the accuracy and fairness of the behavioral interview. "The questions come right out of the assessment. So the candidate's interview is now scored against a pre-existing job profile. I think it's a lot better. And the candidates thought it was fairer.

"The interviews were targeted. We were able to say, here's a dimension, we're going to ask you a question. They, in turn, gave a work-related example to try to show that they've demonstrated that dimension. But in the behavioral interview, though you may give one example, it might encompass all 10 of the behaviors in profile even though you're only asking for one competency." This provides for a rich source of information to determine whether a candidate has the behaviors required by the job profile.

During the internal interviews at the Calgary Police Service, a panel format was used. Although for each rank the panel differed, it would always include one HR person as a monitor. "The interviewers thought it was a huge improvement." Training was a big reason for that feeling. "Training ensured consistency, how to score a behavioral answer. We were able to say, here's how many examples you should get, here's what you're looking at, here's how to compare it against the job profile. That really helped."

During the actual interviews, Dale came up with a unique but completely logical way to make candidates as prepared as possible for the new interviewing style. "I gave all the candidates the questions in advance. Around here, everyone has really good examples from actual work experience." In the old system, the members of the service knew they would always be asked certain questions about the 10 dimensions or competencies being used. "Leadership, for example. All of us would sit around and think, what's my best example, and memorize it. Even if the question didn't come up, you'd fit it in somewhere in the interview. The attitude was, I'm saving this and you're getting it. So you'd end up with a canned response anyway.

"So now, what we've done is, when the interviewers have the initial portion, I send out a package to all the people that are successful in obtaining an interview. The package says, 'You will be asked the following questions pertaining to the following five competencies. However, based on the type of response you give, you're going to have a number of different probing questions.' Of course, they don't know what the probing questions will be, and it's the probing that we've found really brings out the depth in the answers.

"It let us remove some of the stress and puts everyone on the same page. We're saying, 'You're going to get these questions, so give me your best answer.' We find that it speeds up the interview process, and underneath we have a whole series of probing questions all outlined for the panel. They just go down the list and start probing and probing and probing and that's where they found out how good a candidate is. It also helped with some of the people who had weak examples. You could say, 'Alright well what else have you got here,' and probe some more."

Through this interviewing process, one of the goals of the organization was met—to make internal selections more fair, equitable, and merit-based. "People going through the process really felt that the panel was there not to exclude, that it was there to pick out the best. In the old way, we'd ask you a question and that was the end of it. You could ask for clarification and they would read you the question again. There was no feedback. You never knew if you gave a good example or a bad one. The panel used to use the interview process, I think, to eliminate candidates [not select the best]."

Sprint Canada

Victoria Walker says, "The hardest part in the behavioral interviewing process itself for managers is moving away from the old style, away from asking opinion-oriented questions, like what do you think about this or that and what are your greatest strengths..." to a search for behavioral answers. "It's tough for managers to change. Once they do it even in a training session though, they see right away how it's better."

Training, however, was an answer to a deep need managers felt for stronger interviewing abilities. "We found almost unanimously that these managers were hungry for training. They weren't comfortable about interviewing, and they'd never received any training for the most part. So they loved it. For the first time they walked away thinking 'Ok, I feel actually prepared for this. I feel like I might even know how to do an interview.' They were just kind of winging it before, assuming they were doing the right thing because nobody gave them any tools."

This resulted in considerable frustration with interviewing. Managers would wonder, "'Why didn't that person work out?' Or they would walk away and not know if the candidate was good or not. I think we broke down a lot of myths about how those [traditional] questions don't really give you anything." Their reaction was, "'Oh my God, I've been asking those questions for 10 years. Training convinced them. It showed them a new way and then gave them the tools."

The tools, Victoria says, are essential. "If you don't give them the tools and they can't walk right out of that training session and they can't do an interview the next day, it doesn't work. You have to have the tools in place when you give them the training because they need it right away. In a company like ours, they're interviewing all the time."

The interview itself followed the interview guide, moving from must-have competencies, "make-or-break-it stuff" through "a series of behaviors" with two or three questions clustered under each one. Under each question there would be a scoring section, and there'd be a section on the front to culminate all the scoring and develop a grand score, so the guide was a complete tool. You record it directly on the guide, and once you do that, you have your outcome and you have your answers scored—and it can all be passed on to the next interviewer in the process. The next hiring manager could pick another set of questions so that you could, in the end, ask all the questions in the guide.

"What we tried to say to the hiring manager is that a candidate has to earn their way to a behavioral interview. They have to go through the make-it-or-break-it skills questions first. They shouldn't ever be sitting at the table if they haven't gone through with that. You can even do that over the phone. We always encouraged people to do that first and make sure salary is in line before coming to the table for the behavioral interview, because it takes time and is a long process. You wouldn't want to do it and get to the end and find out it was a waste of time."

Training was extensive and detailed. "We trained them on how to probe and dig and get past the barriers such as the vague responses and the 'I don't know, I don't remember' stuff. We went through role plays and all the various scenarios, including how to get to the meat of the interview. We modeled techniques and had them do it. It started as two days of training, and after we got through the bulk of the hiring managers, we took it down to one."

Like the others profiled, she notes that speed and time are a challenge. "In a fast-paced company, there's just never enough time. In some industries two days of training would sell and wouldn't be a problem. But for us, we felt the pressure to take it down to a single day. We didn't want to, but we did it in response to the need." She knows that otherwise the new processes would have been less successful.

The interviews themselves were very thorough. "For the most part, we tried to have multiple interviewers. I was personally involved in a number of sessions with our directors, and they really did go through some beautiful processes. We had nice sequential movements and felt like we had really analyzed these candidates and understood them. It helps a lot if someone who is very trained in the process sits with a less experienced director or manager at the beginning through a couple of real interviews just to demonstrate it in practice, live, because it's hard to break your own habits. I offered that to all the directors in the company specifically when I heard that we were hiring a new director. I'd call the VP and say, 'Let me sit with you. Would you be open to that? Let me go through an interview with you and let me show you how I do it.' Most of them loved it. Some of them said, 'I'll call you back,' and never did. But most were very open to it and it really helped."

Victoria is very clear about the feedback from her hiring managers. "First of all, people needed the tools. They really liked the fact that we developed the interview guides and they were able to walk away saying, 'I've now got some documents; I've got some paper,' or knowing that it was on-line, that they can actually start using it immediately on the very next interview. That immediacy was very important. People told us that time and time again.

"Secondly, the probing questions were also one of the biggest hits. A lot of people would ask the question, listen to the answer, and that's it. They would say, 'You mean I can ask more? I can dig more?' Giving them permission to do that, showing them how to do it without being rude or mean or too overbearing, was very well received. It was something people really liked. They needed to see that in action and do it. You can talk about it forever, but it's one of those things you have to do.

"Finally, the fact that the success profiles were tied to the interview guides showed them how everything worked. They could say, 'Here's my job, here's my success profile, here's my interview guide,' and it all flowed. Our values are at the very top of it all and there's a big cascade there to the jobs themselves. That was really great."

Summary

This chapter has explained the steps involved in conducting interviews so that you can select the best candidate for the job. An in-depth understanding of every aspect of behavioral interviewing—from qualifying potential candidates for interviews to checking references—is essential to success. Behavioral interviewing is a time-consuming process that must be supported throughout the organization if it is to achieve the results you want. But as the case studies so aptly show, all those involved in the process—from hiring managers to HR, from candidates to line workers—reap the benefits. In *Chapter 7: Doing the Numbers: The Right Decision*, we'll turn our attention to making sense of the information you elicit from the interview. Afterall, the purpose is to make the right decision.

Doing the Numbers:
The Right Decision

Suspending Judgment and Developing a Common Language of Assessment

Managers who have been trained in behavioral interviewing frequently comment on how surprised they are by the final assessment of a candidate. Quite often, for example, a candidate who they thought would get high marks does not do as well as expected; conversely, a candidate who would not normally have made an outstanding impression leaps from the pack with a score that demands that an offer be made. Why?

In the traditional interview, many things go through an interviewer's mind—how the candidate's experience matches the job; how he or she compares to other candidates, and how his or her perceived personality, style, background, or biases matches the interviewer's own. All of this creates a strong impression of the candidate's suitability for the job and fit for the organization, but there is actually no data beyond credentials and gut feeling to use in making the selection decision.

To confirm this, take a look at whatever notes are recorded during a typical traditional interview. They will be sketchy at best and not closely reflective of the candidate's actual responses to the interviewer's questions. Often they are in code and overwhelmingly reflect the opinions of the interviewer rather than the actual words of the candidate.

The behavioral interview, on the other hand, forces you to suspend judgment on the candidate until after all the interviews have been completed. It makes you focus on how the candidate compares to the job profile rather than how he or she compares to other candidates. Your detailed notes of the candidate's actual words are compared to the way behaviors are described in the job profile. Points are given for how closely that match is made as well as for how frequently they occur and for how recently the critical incidents have taken place.

For many hiring managers, the scoring process is where the quality of information and the way that assists the selection decision truly reveals itself. Learning how to score remains, however, one of the most challenging aspects of the behavioral interview. It's a skill that requires training and practice as well as a clear understanding of how to make quantitative judgments from qualitative information. It requires that you have and stick with a profile, that you use questions prepared in advance and, most importantly, that you engage the candidate with attentive and active listening which is then reflected in your notes.

For an organization that develops and consistently uses this discipline, the payoff is considerable. Suddenly, the vagaries of top performance are defined in measurable terms that allow a common language of assessment to be used throughout the organization, between managers and with employees themselves as they develop, train, and move into new positions.

The Process

Let's review the stages of conducting the interview and scoring answers.

Going into an interview, the hiring manager has an interview guide in hand. The interview guide describes the job in question through a series of behavioral statements based on the organization's core values and the job's definitions of top performance. The interview questions are designed to generate conversation based on those behavioral statements. The hiring manager asks a series of these behavioral questions and probes the candidate's answers to clarify the critical incidents as well as their underlying behaviors and tangible outcomes.

While the candidate speaks, the interviewer takes detailed notes. After the candidate has left, the interviewer immediately goes over his or her notes to make an assessment of what he or she has learned. Are the behaviors there in the answers? How closely do they match up against the profile? Are they recent? Do they show signs of having been repeated in a number of circumstances? Were the outcomes successful? Evaluating each answer, in turn, forces the interviewer to make a measured judgment of the candidate based only on the job profile. Beside each answer, the interviewer assigns a score based on evidence of the behaviors in question. The scores are totaled, and a picture of the candidate's suitability for the organization and the job is revealed.

Determining Evidence of Behaviors

When conducting the interview and scoring a candidate's responses, the hiring manager must determine not only whether the candidate has exhibited the behaviors required by the job profile but also to what degree he or she has demonstrated the desired behaviors in a variety of previous experiences. To grasp this, we turn to the rule of the Hierarchy of Behaviors. We consider recency, frequency, outcomes, and the similarity of the circumstances in which the behavior was exhibited in the score we give the candidate's answer.

The Hierarchy of Behaviors states that:

1. The more recently a past behavior has been demonstrated, the more likely it is to be repeated

2. The more often the behavior was demonstrated over time, the higher the probability it will be repeated in the future

3. Behaviors that took place in similar circumstances are more likely to be repeated once on the job

Some parameters are important to keep in mind. When a behavior is considered to be recent, it is defined as having taken place in the last 18 months. Examples of recent behaviors should include at least two relevant stories, taking place in the context of very different events, which contain details of the historical context of the critical incident as well as the underlying behaviors and outcomes. Recent behaviors that don't meet this standard are not useful as predictors of future behavior and can be considered one-off events.

Clarity is another vital issue. How clear is the candidate's role in the critical incident being examined? In the ideal circumstances, the role of the candidate should be clearly evident. You can tell that this is the case when the candidate is able to describe his or her role specifically and in unambiguous detail.

It is important, however, to seek "contrary evidence" in order to verify the legitimacy of a behavior that the candidate has displayed. When, as interviewer, you hear repeated evidence of a behavior in a number of circumstances, it is extremely enlightening to seek a time when the behavior was not exhibited. For example, if the candidate has demonstrated in several circumstances that he or she communicates well, ask, with an open-ended question, the candidate to describe a time when, despite his or her best efforts, communication was poor. Not only will you learn a great deal about the real nature of the candidate's ability (in this case with respect to communication), but you may also be able to establish a time line for the development of that behavior. If the occasions when the candidate communicated well are the most recent and the time when communication was a problem is relatively long ago, this might indicate a path of development or an instance in which the candidate learned from an experience.

The goal in a behavioral interview is to establish the pattern of behaviors involved in each critical incident in order to most accurately predict what the candidate will do once on the job. Probe until the circumstances have been fully laid out. You will know when the candidate has been clear and detailed in his or her description when you can see the incident play out like a movie in your mind. In such an instance, the candidate has provided details about what he or she actually did, said, thought, and felt. The story will have been told without hesitation.

Interviewer Beware of:

- Generalizations

- The use of "we"

- Lack of specific time references

- Inability to give a specific person as a reference for a specific incident

- Statement of desired behavior without recent evidence of desired outcomes

---

Scoring Responses: Using the Anchored Rating Scale

For scoring behavioral information we recommend using an anchored rating scale, designed to help you score every aspect of the behavioral profile. This allows the organization to establish a common understanding of how to score each candidate's answers. It permits, no matter how many people are doing interviews and no matter how many candidates are involved, a coordination of the results and a consistent evaluation of each candidate against the profile, not against other candidates. With the anchored rating system, the validity and consistency of the interviewing process is maintained. It is explained in detail below.

Immediately after the interview, you need to assess the candidate's responses based on how closely they match the descriptions of the job profile. Key words are your guide. But remember, the candidate does not have to specifically mention the key word only the behavior. As you listen to the candidate's stories about his or her relevant experiences, make note of when behaviors appear and use probing questions to clarify the circumstances, outcomes, and results. The right behavior that leads to the wrong outcome is not effective. Also, remember to probe for contrary evidence.

Anchored Rating System

An anchored scale is used to score the responses for each dimension of the behavioral profile. Use the following sample to understand how this works.

5	Consistent, recent, and repeated demonstration of all the behaviors	*Within the behavioral dimension the candidate will have consistently exhibited all of the behavioral aspects. There will be evidence of this in recent work and non-work situations.*
4	Recent and repeated demonstration of some of the behaviors	*Within the behavioral dimension the candidate will have consistently exhibited some, but not all of the behavioral aspects. There will be evidence of this in recent work and non-work situations.*

3	Demonstration of the desired behavior in the distant past, in a non-work related situation, or a demonstration of the desired behavior with the wrong outcome	*The candidate will have exhibited the behavior in a work situation at some point though not recently. Or the candidate will have exhibited the behavior in a non-work related situation. Or the candidate will have exhibited the behavior in a work situation but will have failed to achieve the desired outcome.*
2	Theoretical or hypothetical demonstration of the behavior	*The candidate will not have exhibited the behavior in an actual situation but will have answered in a way that shows understanding of the behavior and intent to use the behavior in a theoretical situation.*
1	No evidence of the behavior or understanding of the behavior	*The candidate has never exhibited the behavior. The candidate does not show any signs of understanding the behavior or exhibiting it even theoretically. (This is known as the "mirror" response. Put a mirror under their noses and it will fog up. They are alive but not much more.)*

By totaling the responses related to each dimension, you can see how closely the candidate matches the complete behavioral profile. For many hiring managers, the totaling of a candidate's score can be a surprise and a revelation. Most of us are unaware of how little we focus on a candidate's competencies and to what degree our judgments are subjective. Scoring behavioral answers forces the hiring manager to focus on the job profile, not the personality of the candidate. It is a much more objective, valid, and accurate basis for making a decision.

Case Study Profiles

All of the organizations profiled in this book had positive experiences with the use of an anchored rating system to score behavioral information. While stressing the necessity of thoroughly training interviewers to score accurately, all indicated that scoring remains a nuanced skill that grows with experience.

Calgary Police Service

Dale Burns of the Calgary Police Service compares behavioral and traditional interviews for how they rate candidates. "We used to give about 30 questions and mark the answers from one to five. The first guy to come in, we'd benchmark. If you were the first guy being interviewed you may have given outstanding interviews, but because you were first, I wouldn't know where it should fit. Is he a five or a four? Usually, you'd say something like, 'Well, he's really good so I'll give him a four.' Each candidate who came, the score they got was based on previous candidates rather than the job itself."

Sprint Canada

Victoria Walker of Sprint Canada describes the challenge of getting every hiring manager up to speed on the use of an anchored rating system. "Of all the aspects of the process, this is, in my view, the most difficult thing—you only have a day of training and you could easily spend a half day on scoring alone—and it is very difficult to get all managers to the same level. In the end you are rating people's statements and it is somewhat subjective. The scoring system tries to objectify as much as possible, but you still have fluctuations."

The answer in the short run has been to simplify the scoring system as much as possible. "We tried to develop a very simple kind of way. If you see no evidence of the behaviors, it's this score. If you see some or small evidence, it's this. If you see a good demonstration, score it like this. We tried to make it very simple, just so everyone would be on the same page."

No matter how good an organization's hiring managers are at scoring, there will still be some inaccuracies in who gets chosen. Buyer beware. No selection system can touch on every aspect of a candidate's past. You are not going to get a perfect fit and will still make selection mistakes. But gambling on 70 percent of the information needed to make a good hire instead of 19 percent of the information is a solid mitigation of the risks.

Sample Response Rating

As an example of how scoring takes place in practice, let's look at the responses a candidate gave to questions about the "Networker and Relationship Builder" behavioral dimension from the entry-level engineer profile described in Chapter Four. The behavioral dimension and its concrete depictions are repeated below:

Networker and Relationship Builder

- Works to build or maintain effective relationships or networks of contacts with internal and external associates whose cooperation is important to present or future success

- Uses a variety of methods to influence, persuade, and productively gain others' commitment to ideas, objectives, and changes

An entry-level engineer who is a relationship builder/networker:

- Develops a network of contacts in key departments to facilitate finding the right manager to contact when specific problems arise
- Develops contacts with sister plants to enable the shared development of problems as well as learn from other successes and mistakes
- Develops relationships within the company independently
- Shares the success of the implementation with all those involved
- Finds time to interact with coworkers, formally and informally

The key words for this profile might include: finds right contact, shares learning, develops relationships independently, shares implementation information, interacts formally and informally. Read the questions and answers below; then attach a rating to any segment of the candidate's response which gives some or any of the information needed.

Question:	*Describe a time when you called upon people you know to help you solve a problem.*
Candidate Response	**Rating**
A number of years ago I ended up in quality management. Up to that point my experience had been in human resources and corporate management. I realize that among the people I knew, I did not have contacts who were in this field. So I started identifying who was known to be leading in quality management in the region. This got me in touch with several people who also introduced me to other quality	

practitioners. Through these people I discovered the National Quality Institute. I attended the yearly Awards for Excellence conference where I met quality practitioners and business managers. By participating in a number of workshops, I met several interesting people.	
When I came back I followed up with a number of them, explaining that I was fairly new in the field and could really benefit from their experience. Those that I approached did not hesitate to share their experience. Quickly I came to exchange readings and information that I thought could benefit them as well.	
I also had the chance to work with a world renowned practitioner and author. This individual got me in touch with the European community. I attended a conference in Stockholm with business leaders and quality improvement practitioners from Europe. There I made a number of contacts that I still follow up with today, even though I am no longer in this position.	
I also took the time to map the people in my network. This mapping allowed me to assess the kind of relationships that I have with the people in my network. I find this has helped ensure that I do not rely on just a few people for support or information. It allows me to nurture relationships.	

| **Probe:** | *How different was your approach when seeking information or assistance from internal contacts versus external contacts?* |

| *My approach did not differ. I would say, though, that internally it was easier, since my colleagues and I shared a common understanding of the business we were in. I took the time with both groups, ensuring that I gave back and not just took information, but also provided information before they came looking for it. That way I maintained a two-way dialogue.* | |

| **Probe:** | *Tell me about taking the time to spend with both groups.* |

| *By this I mean that it is important to follow up with people you meet. I find that one of the challenges is having time to do this. I made a point of calling people I met to ask how they were doing or sending them information or an article I thought might interest them. The last thing I wanted to do was call them only when I needed something.* | |
| *I made a point to attend social functions at work. I found that this was one of the best ways to see colleagues you do not work with on a daily basis. Every year I attended the United Way campaign, the company golf tournament and the Christmas party. Once or twice during the week I also tried to go down to the cafeteria and have a coffee with colleagues. I found these informal get-togethers were very productive in terms of information sharing.* | |

Decide on an overall rating for all of the responses taken as a whole. Justify your decision as it relates to the "Relationship Builder/Networker" competency. If you have colleagues working through this book, discuss it with them and then see how others have rated the candidate.

Common Rating and Profile Assessment Errors

It is easy to slip into some ineffective approaches when rating and assessing candidates. It is important to keep an eye out for common rating errors and correct the way you are making assessments should they arise.

After you have completed your rating of a candidate, examine the numbers that you have assigned and determine if you have fallen into any of the common rating errors. If there seems to be a problem, try rating your notes again.

Evaluation errors reflect the average rating that you have given the candidate's responses. These can be of two types. Leniency is demonstrated by offering too many fours and fives. Since not many of us are excellent at everything, you need to determine if this was really an accurate assessment. Take a measured look at your notes again to decide. Toughness, on the other hand, is marked by too many ones and twos. If the candidate has made it to the interview stage, chances are he or she is somewhat qualified. Is anyone really so bad as to deserve all ones and twos?

"Dispersion errors" are a possibility when there is a pattern to the score given for each behavior. Sometimes there are too many threes, and everything about the candidate is marked as average. If this is a tendency of the interviewer, it can make it difficult to differentiate a candidate.

On the other side of the spectrum, some interviewers mark everything in extremes giving ones and fives away rather than taking a measured look at the candidate's answers. It's unlikely that a candidate is excellent whenever he or she displays a behavior and awful whenever he or she isn't as on the mark.

Profile errors are those that reflect the interviewer's rating spread of answers from all candidates combined. You will notice this kind of error after you have rated several applicants. If you notice a tendency to commit profile errors, review your candidate scoring sheets to check out your numbers.

There are two ways in which profile errors are manifested. Halo errors, the tendency to overrate candidates, occur when you have consistently scored a number of candidates mostly as fives. If you see that candidates always have a good score across the same performance topic, you may be committing a halo error for that specific question. Contrast errors are the tendency to rate too many people with nothing but ones or fives. In this case, you are viewing a candidate as either top notch or terrible without discriminating the natural range that exists between them.

During the training session on behavioral interviewing, there should be time set aside to interview other members of the workshop and to score their responses. In addition, you should provide feedback to one another when discussing the answers and scores of actual candidates. It is only through applying the methodology and experience that you will become more accurate and consistent in your evaluation of responses.

The Decision

You have to avoid recommending the person who, in your opinion, is the best. That kind of recommendation is an indication of a comparison to other candidates or a judgment based on personal feelings of like and dislike. Instead, your recommendation for hire needs to take into account in a convincing outline the candidate's overall qualifications by stressing the qualities that impact most on the job.

You have two sources of information for doing this—your notes and your rating of the candidate's answers. Each provides a comprehensive snapshot of that person's ability to perform on the job. This must be complemented, however, by the candidate's entire package. Skills, knowledge, credentials, experiences, and information obtained from other assessment tools and, finally, salary expectations are also important considerations.

No one candidate will be a perfect match. Since all candidates have shortcomings, it will be important to outline what these are. It is equally important to recommend appropriate developmental training to eliminate the potential shortcomings. Because you have compared the behavioral profile to the candidate's behaviors, you will have a relatively accurate perception of any gaps. That knowledge should not be thrown away. You must make your selection decision at least partly on the basis of what the organization can do to support the candidate to be successful on the job.

In effect, this means that the interviewer not only has to be skilled in questioning and evaluating, but also has to be aware of the future training and development that will be necessary for the candidate and the organization to win. Beginning such developmental planning at this stage will dramatically accelerate the recommended candidate's job-level maturity, defined as the point where the candidate is performing independently with minimum supervision and support. You should never make an offer, however, until all of your questions about that candidate have been answered.

Making the Offer

All competitive organizations in a given industry are going to be able to meet the base requirements of candidates. Although there will be some variations, for a candidate entering an industry or switching organizations within it, salary, benefits, and perks will tend to fall within an acceptable range, no matter what company is in question.

You will gain a competitive advantage in making offers if you remember the lessons learned from the McKinsey-Sibson study on the reasons why employees leave organizations. Job satisfaction has less to do with salary than many of us would like to believe. It has everything to do with work styles, organizational values, vision, and culture. A winning offer will sell that complete package to a top-ranked candidate. The candidate who has gone through a behavioral interview will be ready to listen.

An organization's ability to retain its top talent starts right here. The key to retaining talent is to align an employee's values, motives, and drivers with an organization's. The behavioral interview unlocks that information at this crucial time better than any other format. As HR professionals and hiring managers, you have an opportunity to influence the future of your firm at this one time more than at any other. Your hiring decision and your conversation about the offer will have a tremendous impact on your organization's talent edge.

What goes into a selling story?

- Demonstrating the organization's values through actual employee experiences
- Sharing the vision and how each member of the organization makes a contribution to the vision
- Explaining the challenges the organization faces in order to achieve its business plan
- Naming your competition and defining your significant competitive advantages and differences
- Expressing your cultural differentiating factors—why the organization is a good match for the candidate

---

When you are ready to make an offer, have a story to tell the candidate about the values of your firm. "Selling stories" are anecdotes of the organization's key critical incidents. They will contain situations, outcomes, and behaviors which demonstrate the organization's culture, values, and vision. They are the most dramatic and effective way to make your candidate see what it will be like to be a part of your team.

This is true no matter what level of candidate you are approaching. Think about senior executives, for example. They, in particular, are not working for the money any more. Rather, they are looking for the right culture, the right vision. You must sell your vision, values, and culture to them with all the marketing skills at your disposal.

Lead with your strengths. If you have a powerhouse management team, say so. If you have an aggressive commission-oriented employee base increasing revenues year after year, let the candidate know. And be honest about the rest. A realistic job profile will be more appealing to the candidate than a snow-job. It's not just about the first day; it's about the long haul.

Behavioral interviewing will assist you greatly in this process. Your candidate will feel that he or she has a good understanding of the organization when the interview is over. Just as important, the candidate will also feel that he or she has been understood. I have heard of organizations that have candidates who are willing to wait two to three weeks for interviewing results, even with other offers on the table, because of the relationship that has developed through the process of the behavioral interview.

For those candidates who do not accept an offer, send a letter a few months after the fact to ask them about their impressions of your organization, the job they applied for, and the offer. The distance that time creates is powerful and candidates will be both objective and surprisingly insightful. You will see trends over and over in their replies and will be able to adjust your selling strategy accordingly.

With practice, you will realize greater consistency between interviewers in their ability to interpret answers. The importance of providing a consistent anchored rating scale coupled with the specific behaviors of the profile is to give each interviewer a common definition of what to look for in the candidate's responses. Without it, the interviewer will rely on his or her own interpretation and prejudices. If you follow the process, you will be hiring the person with the best fit while providing all candidates a fair, equal, safe, and trustworthy opportunity.

CHAPTER 8

∞

Aligning Organizational Values, Vision, and People: A Common Language of Success

The Hub of the Wheel

The great educator, John Dewey, once said, "Valuation means change of mode of behavior from direct acceptance and welcoming to doubting and looking into—acts which involve postponement of direct (or so-called overt) action and which imply a future act having a different *meaning* from that just now occurring—for even if one decides to continue in the previous act its meaning-content is different when it is chosen after reflective examination."[1]

The essence of learning, in other words, is behaviour change, whether that change involves learning how to use Lotus Notes or how to close a deal. Defining behaviors in relation to organizational values and top performance provides a guide for developing performance mangement, training, coaching, and succession planning systems. For the organization this presents an opportunity for

---

[1] "The Logic of Judgments of Practice" in *John Dewey: The Middle Works*, Volume 8 (1915) p. 30.

greater focus and more targeted development in line with values, vision, and future market strategy; for management it is a clear set of tools and a guideline for having accurate and objective conversations about development and performance; for employees themselves, it represents managment with no surprises and a well-marked road towards success.

All of the organizations researched for this book have seen the value of using behavioral profiles as the hub or core for other HR processes beyond the interviewing process. The reason for this rests in the answer to a simple question. Once brought on, how do you

An Integrated Approach to the Human Resource Planning Process

Selection &
Recruiting

Behavior-Based
Compensation

New Hire
Orientation

Career
Planning

Training &
Development

Behavioral Job
Profile & Values

Succession
Planning

Performance
Management

Individual
Development

encourage those new hires (and indeed others within the organization) to continue focusing on the behaviors that made them successful candidates in the first place? The answer is to encourage, reward, and recognize the behaviors of top performance through your managing, coaching, assessment, reviews, development, succession, and even compensation systems. Doing so creates a common language of success throughout the organization. The power of this cannot be overstated.

I want to conclude by giving a glimpse of the path each of our case study organizations have taken towards extending their use of behavioral profiles into other applications. This will not entail a detailed description, however. Our research into how an organization links its vision and values with its job-level behavioral competencies and overall strategy is only now coming together. That story will be told in a future publication.

Michelin North America

When examining behavioral competency implementation, it is interesting to question how it gets a foothold in the organization.

At Michelin North America, behavioral competencies were initially used in a pilot project to improve the hiring of entry-level engineers through campus recruiting. In order to do this, dozens of focus groups were conducted to determine how the core values of the organization were enacted by top performers. The information was then used to develop a values-driven job profile as the basis for hiring. This resulted in a marked improvement in hiring managers' ability to identify candidates with better fit for the job and the organization.

The highly visible success of this strategy led to important questions from managers—namely, could the criteria for hiring be used also in performance management? Behavioral profiles in place, the organization was ready to move quickly to revamp its performance management system. As has already been described in Chapter Three, the organization had always been divided into two primary groups—managers or professionals and plant employees. These two behavioral profiles, however, showed so much overlap in the way top performance manifests itself on the job that it was determined that using a single performance management system organization-wide was not only doable but a powerful message about success and values.

For plant employees, in particular, it was a recognition of changing expectations. Like many organizations, Michelin was moving towards a more participatory and interactive role in positions that had once been seen as primarily labor focused. Letting plant employees know that all performance appraisals invoked the same core behaviors, regardless if the individual involved was a plant employee, a frontline manager or a second-level manager, changed the criteria and concept of the job.

Later, Michelin went through the process of identifying its core competencies worldwide. Milan Mizerovsky says that the organization is now expected to move towards a competency-based HR system. He feels that the groundwork has been laid for doing just that and that the adoption will consequently have a higher degree of success than that which some organizations have experienced. Employees at Michelin are familiar and comfortable with the concept. They've experienced it and found that it makes sense. Since people were brought into the organization that way, it will be a logical next step to talking about their careers in that terminology too. "If this is what we say leads to success, then it only makes sense that it is also how we should hire, assess, and coach people," Milan says. There's a commonality of language that creates clarity. Nevertheless, though the development of such an integrated approach will be natural, it will still take great effort to put into place and utilize well.

Technology, however, Milan notes, makes it all so much more doable. It will now be possible to use the intranet as a repository of job profiles with their behavioral and technical competencies. Paper-based systems, Milan feels, were too unwieldy for easy adoption in a global organization. Clearly, the next evolution will be to work from on-line profiles; if an employee identifies an area where he or she wants to develop, the online system can, in turn, identify developmental ideas for doing so, whether that involves reading a certain book, attending a course or taking on a project. In other words, Milan says, "Employees themselves can take responsibility for their own development. It becomes very open and takes away a lot of the secrets."

HMV North America

HMV approached its adoption of behavioral profiles from a different angle. As Marnie Falkiner, the former vice president of HMV Canada, described it, HMV went at it from the middle rather than the beginning and worked its way towards either side, first using behavioral profiles in training managers and only later using them in the interviewing process.

According to Marnie, after identifying what successful store managers did, HMV developed a distance-learning package that made new store managers model the behaviors of the most successful store managers for their first 90 days on the job. The "Store Manager's Survival Guide" incorporated the behavioral profile of a successful store manager as those behaviors were actually manifested in common tasks and approaches. The survival guide described what the best store managers do behaviorally when meeting mall management and staff, as well as when coming on the job, how they approach staff and inquire about activities and challenges. It included suggestions for first meetings, ways to get staff excited about other approaches, the history and values of the organization, and technical information such as how to read a P&L report or manage the budgeting process. It was a fully laid-out package that described in concrete behavioral terms how a successful store manager does the job.

The survival guide was made up of blue and white pages. The blue pages were assignments that had to be completed and sent back. The white pages contained the information about behaviors and approaches and were written in language that the store manager would use and find familiar. The descriptions had many anecdotes and stories to describe situations, behaviors, and outcomes. The survival guide became a supplement for the regional manager in a situation where a store could only be visited once or twice a month.

Marnie knew she had a successful tool on her hands when store managers kept asking for copies of "that book" and when district managers brought in were quick to tell her if they thought a store manager in their territory might not have a copy. The survival guide—map for how to do the job successfully—was considered an invaluable resource.

After the development of the survival guide, HMV turned to adopting profiles for behavioral interviewing. With that success, the organization realized that its performance reviews were not up to the same level of quality. They were typical reviews, asking employees what they did well and what they would like to learn in order to foster their careers. Nobody liked doing them, from staff to managers. Out of the entire population only about 20 percent of the people were actually completing and turning them in.

Consequently, HMV developed its performance reviews to reflect the shift to behavioral profiles. Consequently, the performance review form, according to Marnie, became a powerful tool and a means of having "a well-orchestrated conversation that reflected the profile."

Under normal circumstances, using the old review process, a manager and a store staff member would have difficulty discussing important core behaviors such as that person's interpersonal ability, teamwork, or creativity. HMV's store staff were young and individualistic people who were very sensitive to confrontation or a patronizing tone. Merely bringing up an issue in the review often led to a defensive reaction; if the store manager was mentioning it, it must be a problem.

But using the behavioral profile as part of the performance review form eliminated that uncomfortable feeling of confrontation and made it okay to talk about the issues. It was no longer the manager bringing up such topics; it was the form. And because of this, it was widely known that the same issues were being brought up with all employees. The performance management process thus enabled managers to have meaningful conversations with employees that were not personal but concerned the individual's behaviors on the job. The objective format allowed managers to turn what were previously very uncomfortable reviews into constructive and powerful conversations. Employees were compelled to think about their own behaviors as they related to the success profile rather than in comparison to others.

It should be recalled that the average HMV store manager's and employee's first passion is music and that they are not generally college educated. They were in it to be involved in the music industry and they rose rapidly as the company went through rapid expansion. The behavior-focused forms laid out topics in a safe and objective way and provided the participants with the conversational tools that many had not brought with them to the job. The review forms helped them to engage in adult conversation and then provided a guide to conversation beneficial to all parties.

The success of this approach was immediately evident. The return rate of the appraisal forms rose from 25-30 percent to 75 percent. More importantly, the discussions were considered phenomenally valuable by employee and manager alike. Marnie heard feedback such as, "It was the best conversation we've ever had" or "We've never talked about these things before; and I told my manager things that I never have before."

It's important to note that the profile for store employee and store manager was known to both sides. As a result, the store employee engaged in constructive conversation with his or her own managers. This process made the dialogue wide open. It was a sea change in how performance reviews were perceived and valued by both parties. In fact, if anything, the new appraisals went overboard at first. Reviews were lasting up to six hours. Marnie was satisfied that detailed ground was being covered but surprised that it was taking so much time. Typically, when asked how it could possibly last six hours, the participants were equally astonished. "We just got carried away," one said. "Neither of us wanted to stop."

But the sessions were making a huge difference in morale and having an impact on the effectiveness of the stores. They were reinforcing and promoting relationships, giving managers the ability to develop staff, and providing employees with information that was actually going to help further their careers. Over time, after much old laundry had been aired, the reviews settled down to a more reasonable two hours in length before finally reaching a 30-minute duration that seemed sufficient.

As is always the case, the introduction of new performance reviews had been scary at first for those involved. But they understood that it was a logical next step in the process. They already knew the hiring profile, and they had begun to talk the talk of the profile and even reward it on the job before it was adopted into the performance reviews. So the performance review was not as big a leap as it could have been if the groundwork had not already been laid.

HMV was a fast-growing organization and there was a need to induct people very quickly into the culture and the values. A behavioral competency-focused mentorship approach was developed in response to this need. When a new person was hired, someone would be responsible for mentoring him or her into the organization. The behavioral profile was used as the road map for explaining how things worked and what approaches were recognized and promoted.

The bonus program that was in place before the adoption of behavioral profiles had only included managers. Nevertheless, managers were often sharing their bonuses with staff in appreciation of their support and a tacit recognition of their behaviors. The next stage in focusing everyone around the behavioral profile was to extend the bonus program beyond the managers to include the staff. HMV needed staff to behave like a team, to take responsibility, to have an enterprising spirit, and to be open with customers. Identifying the way those values were manifested as behaviors and then rewarding those behaviors made the culture hit home. The bonuses supported the values and behaviors that the organization needed. HMV started seeing a lot of changes in efficiency and profitability. The behavioral approach was both a strong reinforcer of the culture and an effective way to achieve strategy.

Calgary Police Service

Likewise, the Calgary Police Service at first used its work with behavioral profiles in an application other than hiring. The concern that drove the development of the profiles originally was the perception of fairness in the internal promotion system. After the success of that implementation, behavioral profiles were incorporated into hiring and are currently being adapted in the performance management system.

As Dale Burns describes it, "Once we had behavioral profiles in place for various ranks, it was a very easy process to develop a competency-based assessment used for promotional purposes." In a hierarchical organization it made sense to use the profile of the rank an employee was applying to as the standard they should meet. "So, if you are a constable wanting to be a sergeant, it was my view that I may as well assess you for promotional purposes on a sergeant's developmental assessment. I could say, here are the competencies and behaviors that a sergeant should demonstrate. If you want to be one, and you're successful in being promoted next year, that will be your annual assessment. So the promotional assessment for the level below is the actual assessment for the level above."

The performance management system uses those same job profiles but incorporates a combination of self-assessment and coaching to guide and achieve development. From the top, the organization has a business plan committed to different items. The actual implementation of this business plan cascades down to each rank, which, in turn, has its own responsibilities and behaviors. The Calgary Police Service can thus assess each member on how well behaviors are demonstrated. "In a portion of that you must identify two behaviors that you want to improve upon during the upcoming year and that will assist the district or the team in achieving its business plan objectives. In other words, here's what the constables do; here's what I've committed to do to help my deputy. In this way, everyone feels and sees that what they're doing is important and fits with organizational goals."

By concentrating and improving on two behaviors during each assessment period, an employee is not only improving his or her own abilities but also taking concrete steps towards helping the Calgary Police Service realize its community mandate.

Abbott Labs

At Abbott Labs behavioral profiles were always used in the interview guides for hiring purposes. The by-product of switching from an off-the-shelf system to an internally developed competency system, however, was in revamping those profiles for use in performance appraisals, promotions, and succession planning.

Andrée Charbonneau says, "This year, corporately, we're introducing multi-source feedback as part of our performance management program. It's called Performance Excellence. I think I'm going to have an easier time introducing that here than at other affiliates where competencies are not implemented yet. Here, we're really ready."

In the future, merit increases will be based partly on results and partly on the development of behavioral competencies. And succession planning is naturally being looked at from a behavioral competency point of view as well. "When we think a person will be a great candidate for a job, people are saying, 'Okay, let's look at the competency profile for that job and let's look at this person's competencies and see if there's really a match there.'" As Andrée says, "this goes a long way towards taking succession planning from horse-trading talks to intelligent discussions." In training as well, "we look at the performance appraisals and determine that we need to train on certain competencies based on the results."

Because behavioral competencies reduce skills and abilities to their core components, Andrée sees a further important opportunity in people development that will enhance the organization's talent at its top levels.

"Our goal is to recognize the transferability of certain competencies and identify in our structure some key positions where movement between divisions is possible and desirable." The question is, "How do you do that in such a way that you are facilitating movement between divisions in a silo-busting fashion? How can you sift through all these competency profiles and say, 'okay, this is readily transferable and this is unique to this division.'"?

"If you wait too late to cross-pollinate you ultimately promote people to a level where it's very difficult to move them over, because they really don't have a lot of the knowledge and the skills that are required to be effective in the position. And then you run into egos—is the person prepared to go over in a much more junior position to acquire what's lacking? So what we're hoping to do is to identify those competencies that really must be acquired in a particular function or division because they are different than the ones in the other division, in which case, we're really talking about transferability.

"An easy example is in HR. I've had I don't know how many arguments with people, 'Oh we can't consider this person for this position because they don't know this particular collective agreement' and I am always arguing that if the person understands labor relations and has worked with one collective agreement, we should never be holding someone back when they can actually learn the new collective agreement rapidly.

"That's not necessarily the case if you are talking product management, for example, and you are taking someone who has a pharmaceutical base and has a lot of knowledge of human anatomy and antibiotics and those types of drugs and you're wanting to shift that person over to a traditional product or a hospital device where all your background knowledge has got to be totally different."

Understanding the nature of behavioral competencies as opposed to technical skills and knowledge gives an organization clear and useful insights into the talents and abilities of its employee base.

Thomas Cook

While in the Travel Group at Thomas Cook, Christine Deputy was very conscious of the need to develop a fully integrated HR system stemming from the original behavioral profile work. "The idea was to bring employees in with a certain set of behaviors, assess and train them with specific technical skills, then develop and promote them on the next set of behaviors."

To establish an integrated approach, Thomas Cook initially started a behavior-based interviewing system and then proceeded with a performance assessment process that included a multi-source assessment instrument based on the job profile. Later, Thomas Cook did a gap analysis with a group of people to understand the difference between their behaviors and the behaviors for their next role. It all stemmed from the behavioral profile work, a set of clearly articulated statements that provided people with an understanding of what they were doing and why they were doing it.

Christine stresses that "you need to do the due diligence through your focus groups and research in order to understand what are, in fact, the right behaviors for a particular job in your organization at that point in time." Unless you go through the hard work of unearthing those behaviors, your introduction of behavioral interviewing, multi-source feedback, and other performance assessment tools will not make the impact you want and need.

The reaction from managers to the introduction of the new processes was particularly positive. Thomas Cook's approach with these tools was always to work first with the jobs that interacted most intimately with the customer, and then roll back from that into the rest of the organization. When the travel consultant behavioral profile was developed, it allowed managers to have a sense of how to manage these frontline people. In effect, it gave managers a set of guidelines for having a conversation around key topics and knowing what to look for in keeping people on the right course. As they said, "Now I can actually manage this person, understand how to have a conversation with this person, and feel like I know what I'm looking for."

A lot of managers, Christine has observed, manage the way they themselves are, in relation to their own reality, personality, strengths, and weaknesses. This can be very limiting when it comes to supervising or developing employees whose styles are different. "From an HR perspective, you typically hear complaints from managers about an employee's style or attitude or their approach to the job. But nobody can fix that." Using behavioral profiles has allowed the managers at Thomas Cook to focus on concrete aspects of how work is done rather than subjective interpretations of a person's ability.

Starbucks

When she moved to Starbucks, Christine was again challenged to develop an integrated approach to HR systems and once more found that behavioral profiling was the key. "We had a lot of good programs, but they weren't necessarily connected with a common thread. We didn't want to go out and recreate all that again, because a lot of these programs were excellent. What we wanted to do was roll out some kind of overlay to bring everything together."

Starbucks focused on the store manager position and did the profiling work required, then "modified" the programs and language that was already established. Using the profiles as a new and more concrete language for what had always been done enabled HR to pull all systems together into a unified approach.

The goal was a connected system that would help people understand what a career in retail would look like. Providing the behavioral profiles for each position and clarifying the skills and experiences required, then linking those positions to expectations and the resultant pay package took the mystery out of the career path. This helped employees learn how to set goals and objectives for themselves for their own careers, whether it was at Starbucks or another retail environment.

Sprint Canada

For Sprint Canada it all started as a visioning exercise. Before even beginning work on behavioral competencies, they pulled out what they considered to be their best characteristics as indicated by their four core values. It seemed essential to determine what the organization really meant by those values. How were they portrayed in the workplace? How did the best employees exhibit those qualities? Out of those questions, the organization developed a list of what it called its "Values Best Practices." The resulting behavioral profiles— or "Success Profiles" as Sprint Canada termed them—were then used in the organization's behavior-based hiring system and later incorporated into other applications.

Career Quest is an on-line career planning tool that contains all the success profiles in the organization. It uses a question-and-answer technique incorporating a job's behaviors and the organization's values to clarify expectations and requirements. It helps employees look at careers in the company by using the success profile as a road map for self-assessment and development. Employees have reacted very positively to the tool. It's user friendly and accessible from any desktop in the organization. There is a challenge in keeping the profiles up to date in such a fast-paced environment, yet no other approach would be as flexible and reliable.

Next, Sprint Canada developed a brand new performance management tool that uses success profiles as a key piece of information. Sprint's performance management form had always incorporated the organization's values, but in the new version they honed it down into a skills and behaviors approach, assessing both outcomes or results and behaviors. "This was pretty risky," Victoria Walker says. "For a lot of very senior people it was a tough concept to buy." Traditionally, results were all that mattered, yet the new tool now assessed employees on their behaviors as well. They had to be convinced of the importance of behaviors to total fit, but eventually senior management was able to see the value in this approach because the behavioral profiles were concrete statements of the corporation's goals and values. For employees, on the other hand, it all flowed and made sense. They were able to see the logic, according to Victoria, and say, "You did ask me about that behavior in my interview, and I did see it in my profile and now I see it in my performance assessment."

Other programs backed this up. Leadership Edge was used by those nominated as high potentials—those most likely to work through the profile they would need in order to advance into more senior positions. At the executive level, the organization is moving into multi-source assessment based on behavioral profiles as a development tool.

"Recently we drew a diagram," Victoria said. "The success profiles have become the hub of the wheel. The spokes of the wheel are all the key HR programs: behavioral interviewing, coaching and mentoring, career progression, performance management. Everything centers around the core success profiles."

A Final Thought: Championing a Behavioral Approach

Because behavioral profiles are based on an organization's vision and values, they become the DNA, the operating platform, and the frame of reference for how everyone in the organization can think about success and top performance now and in the future. Whether your first application of behavioral profiles is in hiring, promotion, or training, when managers, employees, and executives in the organization see the successful impact of that application, the call will arise to incorporate behavioral tools into additional HR and management systems. Be prepared for the call when it comes.

By making top performance an openly discussed and measured concept, you increase the pressure on everyone to improve in the ways that the organization deems strategically necessary. By hiring, developing, assessing, promoting, and ultimately rewarding by using the concrete terms of behavioral profiles, you sharpen the organization's overall talent edge in the context of its unique values and culture, thus providing that elusive competitive advantage through people.

It's the responsibility of senior management to open the doors for this kind of job-level assessment and overall focus. And it's up to human resources to take full advantage of this opening in order to make a resounding organization-wide impact on how human capital is managed. Doing so provides the tools for managers to hire, train, coach, and assess in more concrete, objective, and productive terms as well as an opportunity for employees to see clearly how the organization defines and measures success and how the individual can achieve it.

In the ever-shrinking world of business, which now crosses cultural boundaries, being able to recognize the desired behaviors is essential to ensuring corporate success in a culturally diverse global economy. As our case studies have clearly amplified, behavioral profiles and their application work regardless of organizational size, mission or business objectives. They enable a fair and accurate evaluation of potential new hires to best fit the corporate culture.

Hiring in a Dot-Com Start-Up: The Tug-of-War Between Growth and Time

Does Hiring Right Work When You're Hiring Fast?

All companies want to hire the best. But could a Silicon Valley start-up in the midst of the dot-com gold rush be strategic about its hiring? And what happens when the gold rush ends?

When we started the research for this book, the economy was running at full throttle and companies in Silicon Valley, in particular, were embroiled in an all-out, bare-knuckled war for talent. Like many others watching the fray, we thought it would be fascinating to look at how a typical high-tech start-up was dealing with the challenge of hiring so many people in such a short period of time to fill their ranks and fuel their growth.

By the time we finished the book, the economic reality for dot-coms had changed drastically. Scores of companies were dead in the water, and the few survivors are currently in a holding pattern, having shifted their strategy from wild expansion and growth to downsizing and a concentration on business fundamentals.

Part of the conventional wisdom about why so many dot-coms failed so fast points to their faulty hiring practices. Whether this belief is based on myth or reality is hard to determine without thoroughly analyzing the industry, but the widely held view is that many dot-coms were founded by young, creative, visionary entrepreneurs who lacked the management skills necessary to take their companies to the next level. Part of what that required, so the thinking goes, was hiring the right people to help them expand in line with their mission, vision, or underlying values.

LookSmart, a leader in Internet infrastructure, in many ways fit the profile of the typical high-tech start-up. It struggled to fill hundreds of openings only a year ago and has transitioned out of blitz mode since, reducing in size and focusing on fundamentals in an effort to ride the storm. Unlike many start-ups, however, LookSmart did make an attempt at structuring its incredible hiring efforts through behavioral interviewing practices.

We interviewed Fran Crisman, director of staffing, to find out why LookSmart became interested in behavioral interviewing, how it took off, what adaptations were made to manage the wild ride, and whether there had been a positive impact on the hiring process as a result. We had a lot of questions that we wanted answered. Namely, would the deliberate, structured approach of behavioral interviewing be seen as doable by CEOs, hiring managers, and recruiters under that kind of pressure? Would behavioral interviewing provide bottom-line value in the short and long term? Would hiring right bolster a company's efforts to separate them from the pack? Here is what we found.

An All-Out Hiring Blitz

When Fran Crisman came on board as director of staffing, she was immediately swamped with the task of fulfilling the tremendous employee staffing demands coming from the business units. LookSmart was a start-up, barely three years old at the time, and moving fast towards an IPO. "Pre-IPO is a very exciting time," Fran says, "especially when your CEO is a real visionary. But it's stressful because you need the people and you need them now. There was nothing here when I came. I had one recruiter and 300 open requisitions. Recs! I had 300 openings. There was no such thing as a rec. There were an enormous number of dot-coms growing around here and as a director of staffing I would almost cry when I heard of another one because I would think, they're going to want all the same software engineers that I want. You get to the point where you'll take anybody."

Up to that time, managers had been hiring on their own through the use of contract recruiters. "There was an extensive use of agencies going on where the manager would just get on the phone and say, "I need this and that" and identify the technical skills required." In general terms, managers knew what kind of person would fit best in the start-up environment, "people who were very entrepreneurial and creative who could work in an unstructured environment, people with high energy who could go forward and be self-managing and self-motivated." But understanding what that meant in terms of concrete behaviors was another matter. There was little conception of how past actions were the best predictor of future performance, nor a firm grasp of which behaviors would allow for success in the immediate present or in the rapidly approaching future.

"The agencies would send people over and we developed a great group of technicians that way, but they weren't necessarily those people who could move up to the next level of being managers," Fran says. "We also discovered that one of the big focuses that we had here, even though we didn't define it at the time, was the ability to work together on a team. So you find in general that in their first year, companies usually bring people on in such a way and in the second year the employee relations issues start. That's when you look around and say, 'You know, we really don't have anyone to be managers.' And sometimes that's only after you've promoted people into a management capacity and realize they can't do it."

First Steps: Easing in a Behavioral Approach

Though Fran had come into the role already a full convert of behavioral interviewing, implementing such a hiring approach was, in the short term, a no-go. "When you bring up behavioral interviewing, people laugh and say forget it. I need Java, I need SKL, and I need them now, and I need someone who's going to do it. They're not even listening to you at this point. They're just going to bang those people in there."

Her first need was to find recruiters to help fill the tremendous number of positions that were open. She tried to kill two birds with one stone by bringing on recruiters with a behavioral interviewing background whenever possible. "My approach was to get very seasoned people in here who understood and could utilize behaviors in their interviews. I was looking for my recruiters to work side by side with managers and slowly ease them into behavioral interviewing."

Still, for the first while, it was a struggle to find the right recruiters. "Early on, I hired two people as contract recruiters who didn't have the same background I had and weren't used to a more structured approach. It didn't work out. Now, as I've gone through and hired my whole staff, I've gotten people who did use structured behavioral interviews, and for those who haven't, I've brought someone in for training."

Developing a staff of recruiters familiar with behavioral techniques helped expose hiring managers to the virtues of a behavioral approach. It was a good first step towards creating some converts.

Seizing the Opportunity to Spread the Word

The opportunity to move more deliberately to a behavioral approach came as the company began the implementation of a multi-rater feedback program called "Smart Feedback."

"Putting together a multi-source instrument in a company as young as LookSmart was a very hard process," Fran says. The development of the Smart Feedback program forced the company, however, to think more clearly about how its vision and values were demonstrated by job actions. It wasn't a stretch to take that work and use it to foster a better understanding of how a behavioral job profile available for assessment could also be used to hire the best candidate in the first place. Fran spun off her own behavioral interviewing initiative from the Smart Feedback program and brought in the outside consultant already working on the assessment instrument to teach courses on behavioral interviewing to anyone who was interested.

"We put out—as you do in start-ups—some really fun e-mails across the company, giving them all the reasons they should come to the behavioral interviewing workshops. But trying to get the managers and those on the interviewing panel to come and give us the time was an extraordinary challenge. We had to beg. We had to borrow. You just couldn't believe it. I had my recruiters out there doing one-on-one selling across the company just to get in the first group."

The secret to the recruiters' success was to sell the course idea to those managers who had already been convinced to adopt some behavioral interviewing techniques. "We had a few faithful that were already converted, people who had been trained on developing questions around core competencies and past experiences. They came to the behavioral interviewing workshop and then helped spread the word."

Some key managers who had been working closely with the recruiters made their entire staff come. "The biggest success we had at the very first workshop was with the vice president of software engineering. He knew that the interviews weren't going right and they needed some training. All his managers were brand new and they didn't know what kinds of questions to ask, and as a result, he was seeing a high level of turnover. We actually got about 20 or so managers and members of that group's interview panels to come and work on developing competencies for software engineers and project managers." Getting wholesale buy-in from one division was a big win for the program.

Adaptations to the Behavioral
Interviewing Workshop

As with everything else at a start-up, time was the most significant
obstacle to getting people to commit to the workshop. "Usually it's
a two-day course," Fran says, "but there was no way we could make
it two days. We had from nine until four to get the message across
and drive home why behavioral interviewing was going to be a
great way to go. Fortunately, it's a very compelling message, and
once you get people to start using the approach on one of their
panels, you're set."

But it was still necessary to take managers beyond mere famil-
iarity with the techniques to a level of sufficient skill in using them.
This was not something that could be accomplished through a sin-
gle-day workshop. Fran realized that hiring managers "needed
someone to follow through with them. They don't completely get
it the first day." Recruiters, therefore, worked directly with the hiring managers and helped to fill out the profile with the behavioral
competencies. They designed the interview questions with the
manager and then led the panels so that each interviewer picked a
certain area to ask questions on. After the interviews, recruiters also
led the feedback on the way the interview was conducted and facilitated the actual decision-making process with panel members to
determine the best candidate. This consensus approach fit with the
way that LookSmart already made its hiring decisions.

To date, LookSmart has conducted five workshops on behavioral interviewing with open invitations for attendance. It was
important, Fran insists, to adopt the style of the workshop to the
culture of an Internet company. The course manual and the interview questions needed to be written to accommodate the target
group of young candidates and embrace the culture and values of
the organization.

Benefits to the Organization: Adapting to Change, Choosing the Right Competencies, and Building a Global Culture

The efforts paid off wherever they were embraced. Behavioral interviewing allowed the organization to be smarter, more strategic, and more coordinated throughout its rapid evolution and across the divisions.

First of all, Fran explains, an Internet start-up is a different kind of environment from most companies. The reality of that needs to be reflected in the kinds of questions asked of candidates. Behavioral questions allow you to target that kind of information directly.

"In sales, for example, just because you've worked well at a Fortune 500 company, doesn't mean you can here. It's a totally different set of values, a totally different environment. When people say, 'Who's going to do that?' you need to look in the mirror, because it's you. There is nobody else. There's no graphics department, no secretaries, nothing. You do it. So how do you elicit from a person's background whether he's going to be able to work in that environment?" Rather than rely on unsubstantiated claims of self-sufficiency, past experiences can be probed for the behaviors that actually indicate such ability.

Also, Fran maintains, the demographic profile of the employees that LookSmart needed required its own special considerations. "Our employee population has an average age of 27 and we have a very entrepreneurial, fast-paced environment. When you're looking at tenure here, it's very short term, and when you combine that with Generation X, you've got a different animal to deal with. We're talking people who join the company and are looking again to move on to something else after six months, because to them its the equivalent of three years."

Behavioral interviewing allowed the organization to be smarter about what kind of employee was needed in the early stages compared to the kind that would be successful after the start-up phase was over. "You find that at that one-year mark they're entrepreneurs and they want to move on. So when you're interviewing during that first year to 18 months, you want entrepreneurial types who want to create. After that first 18 months, you want the maintenance people. They have to be creative, but they have to be able to maintain as well. So you have a different group of people that you're going to be hiring and it's a different environment."

A focus on behaviors helped keep the organization on track despite constant change. "You always have to be able to adapt in an Internet company to the new strategy. It's not like at Ford or GM where you can put together a business plan for the year. Every quarter there's some kind of new strategy that you're doing. I laugh when I think of last year when I put together my budget and said that we were going to hire a maximum of 200 people with 25 percent turnover, and we actually hired 500 people." Using behaviors as a reinforcement of strategy and culture gave consistency to an organization undergoing so much growth and change. As Fran puts it, "You're continually training people and absorbing them into the organization and ensuring that as managers they can embrace the values and actually hire the right people."

The second benefit of behavioral interviewing was in the way it focused the organization on the fundamental competencies required to be successful in LookSmart's culture. In particular, teamwork was discovered to be absolutely key. As Fran describes, "Here at LookSmart, it doesn't matter whether you're in marketing, engineering or sales, in order to be successful at your job, you have to work across all the teams. The ability of employees to participate as team members in their own groups and across departments is extraordinarily important to our success." As proof, she points out all the people who work on a web page created by LookSmart. "Someone has sold that page to the customer. The product group has designed it. The engineering group has put the application behind the scenes. The editors are doing the copy on it. Business development originally put the deal together. So whoever's managing across those teams has to be able to communicate effectively, process manage very well, and be influential with people that are generally pretty creative and fast-paced in their own right. Those people, in turn, have to influence the other members of their own teams to come together as a group to get that product out as quickly as possible, all so sales can meet their obligations and we can bring the revenue in to become profitable. Because, like every other dot-com out there, if we're not profitable in the second quarter we're going to go down the tubes."

It's only by determining how those competencies such as team work, creativity, an ability to meet deadlines, and analytical thinking are defined in concrete behavioral terms that the organization has a shot at picking the right people. "When you define those competencies and develop the profiles, it's like 'Aha!'" Fran says.

Finally, a behavioral approach helped the organization dedicate a common standard to hiring internationally, across cultures. The Internet may be a global communication system, but staffing a global start-up can be a daunting task. Given the cultural gap that needed to be overcome merely to hire Generation X employees who were American, it seemed an even greater challenge hiring young people who were French Canadian, Japanese, German, Norwegian, or Brazilian to open branches of the company abroad.

As Fran describes it, "When you're interviewing internationally, you worry that your approach is not going to adapt to those cultures."

They did have to make cultural adaptations, but only in terms of style, not with regard to the basic characteristics of a successful LookSmart employee. To anticipate and accommodate cultural differences, Fran and others worked with the recruitment team leaders in each country to develop questions that took cultural values into account.

The competencies that made for a successful LookSmart editor in the United States or Australia were, however, the same competencies that led to success in France, Germany, or Brazil. Fran had to strongly emphasize that point with her recruiters overseas. "People said we can't use those kinds of questions in Japan." But it was important to emphasize that "it's really not an invasion of privacy. People will share this kind of information." Rather than being a difficult launch, the Japan office became an example of how well behavioral interviewing worked. "We were wildly successful in opening that office in Tokyo. We hired that team probably the fastest of all the countries even though I had the most trepidation about it. We had it up and running in just a few months." Despite cultural differences, the behavioral interviewing process helped the Japanese recruiter narrow down and identify the basic competencies needed in her candidates to achieve success implementing LookSmart's business model.

How Hiring Managers and Senior Executives Have Embraced the Process

Fran admits that the use of a strict behavioral interviewing approach remains an ongoing journey. Much of that difficulty can be attributed to the fast and loose culture that makes an Internet start-up exciting and capable of dramatic growth in the first place.

"It's fun and exciting and we're just here to help managers hire the right people and give them the best tools, but it's a much different sell here, harder to be honest. I was at Qantas Airlines and Southern Bell Communications and brought behavioral interviewing into those companies, and it was easier because it was mandated. You had to go to behavioral interviewing workshops. You had to use it. It made life a lot easier for me. When managers became managers, there were courses they had to go to. And it was easier to convert the VPs there because we had more time. It's not like at an Internet company where people are already running on a 24-hour clock and being asked to fit one more thing in."

At a company like LookSmart, nothing is ever going to be mandated. "No one's going to say you have to do this; they're going to say it's recommended. You can provide the tools and point out the opportunities to use them, but it's more about influencing people, saying 'try this.'" That's why it remains so important for recruiters to work closely with hiring managers with whom they have one-on-one relationships and constantly reinforce the concepts to help spread the word across the company.

There are gaps in the process. Some managers, Fran admits, "skip steps." In one division, for example, the approach has been embraced and is being used very successfully, despite a difficult employee market. In a different division, however, the new vice president came to Fran to discuss his concerns. "He said, you know, we have interviewers and when I sit down to discuss with them what information they've gathered out of the interview process, they don't really have anything concrete to share." Fran explained the principles of behavioral interviewing to the new vice president, and he quickly agreed to hold another workshop and go over those principles with his hiring staff in order to reinforce the behavioral approach.

To be honest, Fran says, even if recruiters and hiring managers don't embrace a completely structured approach, a simple understanding of the concepts is not without benefit. "They know how to develop questions, they understand that past behavior is the best predictor of future performance. So you know they're not going to just run through a résumé without thinking about what that candidate has done in the past."

Although organizationally it is still a bottom-up movement and has yet to be fully embraced at the top, behavioral interviewing is now being slowly incorporated into the hiring decisions for the senior leaders of the company as well. Fran says that her own boss, the vice president of human resources, is working very closely with the CEO and senior leadership team to look at turnover and how hiring decisions are made. The "Aha," she says, is starting to happen and she is seizing all opportunities to coach or convert members of the senior team.

"I just sat with one of our senior vice presidents and he was going to check references on someone. We were talking about the behavioral competencies needed for the job, what performance skills are really necessary, and he said, 'you know Fran, I know all about this guy, I've known him as a friend, all the senior leadership team has interviewed him, but when I ask him if he can close big deals, I don't feel I know whether he can do that.'"

Working closely with that senior vice president, Fran helped to identify what he was really looking for in terms of concrete behaviors that might be gleaned from the candidate's past experiences. "I coached him so that he could focus on what the candidate had done in the past, and the next day he came back and said it had been great. He started rattling off what he'd done with other companies." Another convert had been made, another breakthrough achieved.

Conclusion: a Step-by-Step Approach

It is important to note that behavioral interviewing will not assist companies that are overly focused or intent on hiring first and foremost for technical expertise. But in order for behavioral interviewing to succeed even when intentions are good, an understanding of the importance of organizational values and culture must be part of the mix.

Focusing on technical expertise when hiring without linking the job in question to behavioral competencies is not a stable way of building a company. It will result in the hiring of a wide variety of employees, who, while they might be able to do the job technically, will probably not achieve the desired performance results because of interpersonal conflict.

LookSmart recognized this and made efforts to institute the right behavioral approach. Fran Crisman and the vice president of human resources had a vision for behavioral interviewing that was not, unfortunately, consistently deployed throughout the organization. As a result overall success was perhaps mixed. As Fran relays it, converting an Internet start-up in mid-stream to a more rigorous hiring approach was not without its hurdles. But it was necessary, no matter what, to progress from a stage in which anyone with the requisite technical skills was acceptable to one in which people were being chosen who were capable of executing the overall corporate vision.

While we cannot directly suggest that the many failed dot-coms had their difficulties because of inconsistency in hiring, it seems likely that those who survived have done so because the strength of their culture was reflected in the employees they brought on board.

High-tech companies in particular are susceptible to the expediency demands of rapid growth. Anyone initiating a behavioral approach in such an organization must have credibility with hiring managers and senior leaders in order to influence their methods. Fortunately, the logic of selecting for behaviors is a compelling argument for being more strategic about the hiring process. With every convert comes the opportunity to spread the word and create more converts. A focus on behaviors helps managers reduce turnover, determine the competencies required for top performance and identify the candidates with the best fit for the organization. Inevitably, the behavioral approach therefore becomes the basis for a common language of people practices. Nevertheless, it's up to the leaders in human resources in both corporate headquarters and in the field, to use their influence and persistence to build support for the approach.

Index

ଈଏ